Selected Writi

Volume I

Best wishes
Kerry
Kerry Underwood
March 2016

Kerry Underwood

To

My Niece

MARIE

Law Abroad PLC

First softback edition printed 2016 in the United Kingdom.

A catalogue record for this book is available from the British Library.

ISBN 978-0-9935349-1-1

Published by Law Abroad Publishing, part of Law Abroad PLC

For more copies of this book, please email: d.barnard@lawabroad.net

Tel: 01442 430900

Designed and set by Law Abroad Publishing, part of Law Abroad PLC, 79 Marlowes, Hemel Hempstead, Hertfordshire, HP1 1LF

http://www.underwoods-solicitors.co.uk/

Printed in Great Britain by Halstan & Co Ltd, 2-10 Plantation Road, Amersham, Buckinghamshire, HP6 6HJ

THANK YOU!

Special thanks to:

Doné Barnard
Jamiel Zaman

Thanks to:

British International School of Stavanger, Norway
Claims Magazine
New Law Journal
Solicitors Journal
Malcolm George
Phoebe Ranger
Stuart Thompson
Andrew Twambley
My blog subscribers
My followers on Twitter

"It's the same each time with progress. First they ignore you, then they say you're mad, then dangerous, then there's a pause and then you can't find anyone who disagrees with you."

Tony Benn

"If you don't know where you are going any road will take you there"

Lewis Carroll: Alice in Wonderland

The Author

Kerry Underwood is a solicitor and is senior partner of Underwoods Solicitors. He is a lecturer, writer, broadcaster and former Employment Judge.

Kerry writes and edits the Costs and Funding section of Butterworths Personal Injury Litigation Service and is a regular contributor to Litigation Funding, New Law Journal, Solicitors Journal, Claims Magazine and the Law Society's Civil Justice Section Newsletter.

Former Councillor and Parliamentary Candidate.

Kerry travels extensively and home is his beloved adopted town of Hemel Hempstead. Underwoods Solicitors sponsor Hemel Hempstead Town Football Club and Hemel Stags Rugby League Club.

Interests include football, cricket, gardening and reading. Kerry still plays cricket and is Chairman of his village club Bovingdon Cricket Club.

Nelson Mandela, TS Eliot and Elvis are amongst his heroes.

Kerry supports Queens Park Rangers.

 Follow @kerry_underwood

See Kerry's blog at: kerryunderwood.wordpress.com

Other titles by Kerry Underwood

Qualified One-Way Costs Shifting, Section 57 and Set-Off
Small Claims, Fixed Costs and Portals
Wasted Costs and Third Party Costs
Litigants in Person
Court and Tribunal Fees and Remissions
Conditional Fee Agreements, Damages-Based Agreements and Contingency Fees
Selected Writings Volume 2

Non – Law books

My Dad and Other Pieces

CONTENTS

INTRODUCTION

This first volume of legal writings is drawn from pieces published on my blog and in New Law Journal and Claims Magazine and Solicitors Journal and I am grateful for their permission to reproduce them here.

This book also includes pieces written for Claims Magazine by my good friend and fellow legal commentator Andrew Twambley and I am very grateful to Andrew for allowing their inclusion here.

Some are serious, some less so.

The first section, literally deadly serious given the numbers of avoidable deaths at the hands of the National Health Service, looks at the National Health Service Litigation Authority and its less than truthful reports to Parliament.

The second section looks at the disreputable and downright immoral and illegal activities of some, and I stress the word some, insurance companies. What sticks in the throat of many of us is the way that the insurance industry has persuaded the government that claimants are fraudsters and that they are angels protecting the insurance premium payers.

Nothing could be further from the truth.

The third section has pieces involving my fictitious legal journalist Dick Chilblain. Dick started as a parody of certain legal journalists but those journalists' musings are now such that they have become a parody of Dick Chilblain.

I hasten to add that the vast majority of legal journalists are talented, know their stuff and understand the importance to society of the rule of law and lawyers, while not being blind to the shortcomings of the system, particularly in relation to costs.

The fourth section, Miscellaneous pieces – is just that and deals with subjects such as pro bono, Employment Tribunal fees, the Civil Procedure Rules

Committee, the Civil Justice Council and the Legal Ombudsman and mediation in personal injury cases.

I am not very fond of any of them.

Kerry Underwood — March 2016

2016: SOME PREDICTIONS

Fred, who once stepped in at short notice to take the minutes at the Rutland West Junior Lawyers' Division Social Events subcommittee, will be the Law Society Gazette's Legal Personality of the year.

Approximately 638 lawyer wannabees who could not be bothered passing the exams will announce new systems of delivering law.

Each will be a game changer.

Each will be reported in banner headlines by the Law Society's Gazette. Each will be run by people who have failed and failed again running legal services providers.

Each will fail.

10 000 firms of solicitors will carry on serving their communities and that service will hardly get a column inch in the legal press.

Claimant personal injury lawyers will huff and puff about the small claims limit rise and everything else but in fact will quietly readjust, refocus their businesses and carry on successfully.

Personal injury defence firms will be in very serious trouble; it is hard to see many surviving.

After-The-Event insurance will largely disappear.

The scrapping of general damages in soft tissue cases will run into difficulties in Parliament.

Qualified One-Way Costs Shifting will become the big costs issue.

Three people who have never practised law, most of them from the same family, will tell the 200 000 of us who do how we should do it and will tell us that it will all be done by Artificial Insemination, or something like that.

62 million Britons will still want to see lawyers and doctors, rather than computers.

Motor insurance premiums will not fall.

It will be made illegal to claim against any motor insurance policy for anything.

Motor insurance premiums still do not fall.

Being injured becomes a criminal offence.

Motor insurance premiums still do not fall.

George Osborne and Jack Straw form a new political party: The Insurance Company Party.

Motor insurance premiums still do not fall.

The world ceases to exist

Still motor insurance premiums do not fall

Queens Park Rangers will not be promoted.

Section 1

The National
Health Service
Lying Authority

THE NATIONAL HEALTH SERVICE LYING AUTHORITY (NHSLA)

The National Health Service Litigation Authority describes itself on its website as "a not-for-profit part of the NHS. We manage negligence and other claims against the NHS in England on behalf of our member organisations."

The National Health Service is a wonderful concept.

The National Health Service Litigation Authority is not. It should be broken up.

The pieces appearing here have appeared as posts on my website and have not been published elsewhere.

In late 2015 and early 2016 two court decisions demonstrate the judiciary's frustration with the NHSLA, with the courts ordering indemnity costs against them.

The Parliamentary and Health Service Ombudsman put together a damning report on 22 September 2015.

Research published by the Foundation on 13 January 2016, but dealing with data only to 2013, and sometimes only to 2009, showed that the proportion of successful claims against the NHSLA increased from 45% to 70% between 2001 and 2009 "possible because" no win, no fee lawyers were more cautious about taking on risky claims than the Legal Services Commission (formerly responsible for the legal administering aid).

At the end of this section is a list of sources. If you go to my blog related to this book – Selected Legal Writings Volume 1 – you will see listed the sources for the pieces. By clicking on the link you can access all of the NHSLA reports and the Nuffield Research.

Judge for yourself whether the NHSLA is fit to exist.

NHSLA 2014/15: ANOTHER DISINGENUOUS REPORT TO PARLIAMENT

In its Annual Report to Parliament, published by the House of Commons on 16 July 2015 the National Health Service Litigation Authority has its annual whinge about lawyers acting for claimants that the NHS has negligently killed or injured.

In 2013/14 there were 174,872 written complaints to the Health Service Ombudsman. I must have carelessly overlooked this in the NHSLA's report to Parliament – surely they would not have left this out.
The report of the Parliamentary and Health Service Ombudsman dated 22 September 2015 showed that in relation to acute trusts complaints rose to 21,370 as compared to 18,870 in the previous year, that is a rise of 13.25%.

The NHSLA report states that claimant costs for lower value claims are disproportionate and excessive but boasts of the number of matters it has taken to Detailed Assessment.

It says:-

"The reality is that we can exert only limited control over a claimant's legal costs and no control at all where those costs are incurred before the claim is even reported to the NHSLA."

That gives the clear impression that claimants' solicitors can charge what they want, without any checks.

The truth is that the NHSLA can have every single bill assessed by the court. Why it does not do so and thus allow the court to control the costs, which is the function of the court and not that of the claimant or the NHSLA ,will become apparent when you see what the courts have had to say recently about the conduct of the NHSLA.

The NHSLA cannot really believe that costs judges are routinely allowing excessive and disproportionate costs. Is this not another political move by a politically motivated body to skew the data ahead of Parliament's consideration of fixed costs in clinical negligence cases?

The NHS LA has a history of this and presented similarly misleading data when the abolition of recoverability of success fees and ATE premiums was being considered by Parliament.

Its statement on page 20, that I have just quoted, is hardly consistent with its statement on page 6:-

"This year we contested a high number of cases to trial and challenged numerous claims for claimant costs at detailed assessment, achieving significant savings for our members."

Maybe. Nuffield Foundation Research published on 13 January 2016 shows that between 2001 and 2009 the proportion of successful claims against the NHSLA, or its "members" jumped from 45% to 70%, although it does state that the increase may now have stopped, or even been reversed.

The courts have been less happy with this "fight at all costs" tactic and twice in the last two months have taken the rare step of awarding indemnity costs against the NHSLA for its conduct of litigation, specifically its failure to mediate. In an age of budgeting and proportionality indemnity costs are very much higher than standard costs so that policy is costing, not saving, the NHSLA – you and me as it is taxpayer funded – money.

The language and tone is Orwellian. It cannot force itself to say that the number of claims has dropped – by 3.76% from 11,945 to 11,497 in the last year, but rather says:-

"We received 11,497 new clinical negligence claims in 2014/15 demonstrating a sustained high level of new claims."

It refers to a "slowdown in growth". No, a drop in the number of claims is not "a slowdown in growth". It is a *drop*.

The rise in the percentage of successful cases appears in the Nuffield research and not in the NHSLA report. The Nuffield research states that the increase in success rates is "possibly because "No Win No Fee" lawyers are more cautious about taking on risky claims than the Legal Service Commission (formerly responsible for administering legal aid). "

Pretty obvious really.

In The Year in Summary on page 14 there is a pretty little wheel – figure 13 –

"Damages and costs saved in clinical negligence claims resolved in 2014/15"

And this includes subsections as follows:-

- Successfully defended at trial

- Resolved without damages payable

- Legal costs challenged and saved.

Of the £ 1.32 billion apparently "saved" just £ 38.6 million, that is 3.74% *including damages* is "saved" by going to trial.

Curiously no wheel appears showing the massive costs incurred unnecessarily by the NHSLA as a result of the incompetent, aggressive and unreasonable defence of its claims. I bet it comfortably exceeds the £38.6 million, which of course includes damages, allegedly saved.

On page 8 the report lists eight factors as "drivers" of the costs of claims. (See below)

However a look at figure 1, not mentioned in the eight drivers, shows that claims received as a percentage of NHS activity have dropped sharply, suggesting that lawyers are correctly identifying the cases which should be brought, as evidenced by the jump in the percentage of successful cases.

Thus the true picture is that claims against the NHS are falling, that a greater percentage of those brought are successful and that claims lodged as a percentage of the NHS activity have dropped sharply.

Thus if there are any concerns then those concerns are that due to the abolition of legal aid, except in very limited circumstances, in relation to clinical negligence and the huge hike in court fees genuinely injured claimants are unable to pursue claims.

The NHSLA's statement on page 19:-

"We have always sought to resolve claims without litigation, and we continue to use a range of alternative dispute resolution options in appropriate cases, including formal mediation."

will make any clinical negligence lawyers laugh out loud, or weep, or both.

Pages 25 to 27 have some selected, favourable, quotes from judgments in the NHSLA's favour. Here are some from this year which I am not expecting to be in next year's report to Parliament:-

"9. In respect of the Defendant's failure to mediate, I think the only sanctions available for me to impose are to award costs on the indemnity basis and to award interest on those costs from a date earlier than today, today being the normal date. I am persuaded that the defendant's refusal to mediate in this case was unreasonable. It took them six weeks to reply to the offer and they then replied in the negative...

12. If the party unwilling to mediate is the losing party, the normal sanction is an order to pay the winner's costs on the indemnity basis and that means that they will have to pay their opponent's costs even if those costs are not proportionate to what is at stake. This penalty is imposed because the court wants to show its disapproval of their conduct. I do disapprove of this defendant's conduct but only as from the date they are likely to have received the offer to mediate."

Read v Buckinghamshire Healthcare NHS Trust [2015] EWHC B21 (Costs) 28 October 2015

In Bristow v The Princess Alexander Hospital NHS Trust – case number HQ12X02176

the NHSLA was ordered to pay indemnity costs for the entire proceedings following its rejection of an offer to mediate the costs of a dispute.

Master Simon said that the parties "should be encouraged to enter into mediation, and if they fail to do so unreasonably then there should be a sanction… they gave no good reason other than the fact that the case had already been sat down for a Detailed Assessment".

The case was brought by Irwin Mitchell and one of their partners, Tom Blackburn said that despite the ruling in this case and in *Read v Buckinghamshire* the NHSLA had not changed its tactics

"We had this ruling at the beginning of November, and we have still not had one mediation.

Insurers have been slow on the uptake, but have accepted mediations in some cases. They care about their bottom line."

In neither case has the NHSLA appealed.

Here are the comments from the Parliamentary and Health Service ombudsmen on 8 December 2015 which I am not expecting to see in next year's report to Parliament either.

"Nearly three quarters of hospital investigations into complaints about avoidable harm and death claimed there were no failings in the care given, despite the Parliamentary and Health Service Ombudsman's investigations of the same incidents uncovering serious failings.

The wide range in review of the quality of NHS investigations into complaints about avoidable harm of death by the Parliamentary and Health Service Ombudsman, found that inadequate hospital investigations are leaving distraught patients and families without answers and delaying much needed service improvement. "

The Ombudsman found that:

-

- "Nearly three quarters (73%) of cases where the Parliamentary and Health Service Ombudsman found clear failings, hospitals claimed in their early investigations of the same incident that they had not found any failings.

- Hospitals failed to class more than two thirds of avoidable harm cases as serious incidents, meaning that they were not properly investigated.

- 19% of NHS investigations were missing crucial evidence such as medical records, statements and interviews.

- 36% of the NHS investigations which recorded failings did not find out why they had happened, despite 91% of NHS complaint managers claiming that they are confident they could out answers. "

"Parents and families are being met with a wall of silence from the NHS when they seek answers as to why their loved one died or was harmed. "

"Our review found that NHS investigations into complaints about avoidable death and harm are simply not good enough. They are not consistent, reliable or transparent, which means that too many people are being forced to bring their complaint to us to get a result. In the period 1 January 2015 to 1 December 2015 the Parliamentary and Health Service Ombudsman investigated 536 cases about potentially avoidable deaths and upheld the complaint in relation to 264 avoidable deaths. "

The report states on the front:-

"Ordered by the House of Commons to be printed 16th July 2015"

I look forward to the day when an Act of Parliament says:-

NHS Litigation Authority

"Ordered by the House of Commons to be abolished."

Drivers

1. An increase in the number of patients being treated by the NHS.

2. An increase in the number of reported incidents. This may indicate an increasing and positive reporting culture and so is not necessarily reflective of an increase in incidents occurring.

3. An increase in the number of patients claiming compensation as a proportion of reported incidents.

4. An increase in the number of patients who claim but who do not recover compensation.

5. An increase in the number of lower value claims.

6. Disproportionate claimant legal costs for lower value claims.

7. Excessive claims for legal costs from some claimant firms.

8. Rising lump sums and annual costs (usually, for care), over and above inflation, for high value claims.

THE NHS LYING AUTHORITY AT IT AGAIN

The NHS Litigation Authority is at it again – doing what it is best at – misleading Parliament.

In its Annual Report to Parliament and accounts 2013/14, July 2014, the NHSLA states that it "dealt effectively with an unprecedented increase in claims" (Page 18).

That "unprecedented increase" was 17.9%, on the NHSLA's own figures, in new clinical claims in 2013/14 as compared with 2012/13.

The Oxford English dictionary definition of "unprecedented" is:

"Adjective: Having no precedent, unparalleled; that has not previously occurred".

In its 2010/11 report to Parliament the NHSLA said:

"After large increases in previous years we saw new claims volumes for newly reported clinical claims rise by around 30% in 2010/11 and by around 6% for non-clinical".

How, on the NHSLA's *own figures* is 17.9% "an unprecedented increase" when, on the NHSLA's *own figures* the increase in 2010/11 was "around 30%"?

In my blog NHS Litigation Authority: How it misled Parliament I demonstrated that there was never any such increase and that the true figure was around 7.5%.

Now it is true that based on the true previous figures a genuine increase of 17.9% may indeed be "unprecedented" but the NHSLA has never resiled from its misleading earlier report. By its own figures the NHSLA was lying then or is lying now.

Any which way let us assume that there has been a 17.9% increase; that is undoubtedly significant. May there be an explanation other than a rampant, solicitor fuelled upsurge in compensationitis?

Yes, actually. Tucked away on page 18 appears:

"This significant increase in the number of claims coincided with the Legal Aid, Sentencing and Punishment of Offenders Act (LASPO) coming into effect on 1 April 2013. This legislation, including changes to "no win – no

14

fee" arrangements, stopping claimant lawyers charging up to 100% success fees on their costs and banning referral fees.

Prior to LASPO, we saw significant marketing campaigns by claimant solicitors to ensure claimants signed up to pre-LASPO no win – no fee arrangements, which still enable claimant solicitors to charge a success fee on their costs. As a result, the vast majority of claims reported to us throughout the year have been conducted under the pre-LASPO arrangements".

Quite. Thus there has been an *acceleration* of claims, but not necessarily an unusual or "unprecedented" increase over and above the usual 7% to 10% annual increase.

Incidentally in its 2010/11 report the NHSLA said this:

"We are delighted that the Ministry of Justice is taking forward the recommendations made by Lord Justice Jackson regarding the costs of civil litigation. We believe very strongly that a regime which allows success fees and the recoverability of after-the-event (ATE) insurance premiums makes litigation so profitable that solicitors and so-called "claims farmers" are drawn into the market thereby fuelling the rise in claims volumes we have experienced".

Be careful what you wish for.

The Report itself recognizes that this is likely to be a one-off distortion.

"In the shorter term the introduction of LASPO has increased the number of claims received by the NHS under pre-LASPO funding arrangements" (Page 27).

It appears not to occur to the NHSLA that even this relatively modest increase may be caused by increasing negligence by what is at times a dysfunctional body. No negligence = no successful claims.

Next year's report is easy to forecast. Claims will be up again and the given reason will be that Qualified One Way Costs Shifting allows anyone to bring a claim free of risk.

Oh, in case you did not notice it among the hysterical headlines the total expenditure by the NHSLA on clinical negligence and non-clinical claims *dropped* in 2013/14 as compared with 2012/13.

One of those hysterical statements was from the Medical Defence Union that hospital claims could cost each taxpayer at least £1,000 a year if inflation continues at the current pace.

In 2013-14 the total cost was £1.244 billion, that is £20.74 per UK resident.

I won't work out the cumulative effect of inflation but at a straight 3% the cost will rise by 62p per year and it will take 1,613 years before the annual costs will reach £1,000 per person, that is the year 3627.

How about you stick to medicine and leave the truth to lawyers?

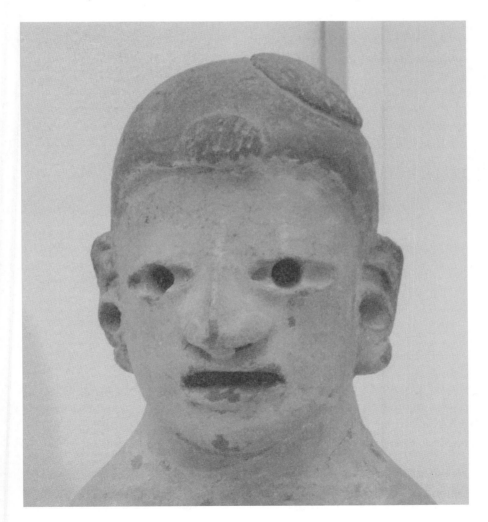

NHS LITIGATION AUTHORITY: HOW IT MISLED PARLIAMENT

One year ago I wrote about the 2010-2011 NHSLA Report to Parliament and suggested that its statement that "after large increases in previous years we saw new claims volumes for newly reported clinical claims rise by around 30% in 2010-2011" was misleading and that the truth was very different.

The press picked up on the NHSLA statement and lurid headlines followed with this being used as yet another example of the compensation culture.

I said then that "No such increase ever occurred" and that the true figure, based on other statistics was between 6.67% and 7.51%, an increase indeed, but consistent with previous increases.

The reason behind the apparent increase was a change in the reporting methods, something tucked away on Page 12 of the report, whereas the headline figure was contained in the opening statement of Mr Steve Walker, the then Chief Executive, but no longer in that position.

I said:

"Of course next year, based on this year's higher figure and using the same, new, recording procedure the percentage increase will revert to a true figure, so it is just this one year when the percentage increase is distorted upwards".

Now it is next year and the 2011-2012 Report has been published.

Was I right?

Yes. This year's report shows that the number of new claims rose by 6% with clinical claims rising by just 5.6% and non-clinical claims by 6.3%.

These figures are very similar indeed to last year's true figures, and actually show a slight drop in the rate of increase in the number of claims, and indeed this year's report recognizes that this year's increase is "lower than each of the previous three years" (Page 11).

Nevertheless, Mr Tom Fothergill, Director of Finance, persists with the fiction that there was a large rise in claims last year, saying:

"The number of new claims received in the year rose by 6%, a significant increase but a substantially lower one than in 2010-2011." (Page 11) and

"As the graph indicates, clinical and non-clinical claims grew at a similar rate (5.6% and 6.3% respectively) after the sudden sharp rise of over 30% in clinical claims in the year before" (Page 11).

Mr Fothergill, like Mr Walker before him, knows full well that there was no "sudden sharp rise" – indeed he goes on to say:

"Part of the growth in claims volumes in recent years is attributable to the earlier reporting of claims….".

In fact the whole of the apparent additional jump last year, over and above the rise of 6% or so, is explained by a change in the reporting system.

Misleading Parliament is a very serious matter. In this case it is even more serious than normal as the misleading 2010-2011 Report to Parliament was the current Report throughout the period that Parliament debated and voted upon the Legal Aid Sentencing and Punishment of Offenders Bill, which became law 3 months ago. That Bill, now the Legal Aid, Sentencing and Punishment of Offenders Act 2012, largely abolished legal aid for clinical negligence cases and also, through abolishing recoverability of conditional fee success fees, made it far harder for claimants to bring claims.

I am not saying that the outcome of the Parliamentary debates would have been different had this misleading report not been published.

I simply do not know. However, we all know that this was a highly controversial Bill which suffered a record number of defeats in modern times in the House of Lords.

I am not expecting banner headlines in the Daily Mail or The Telegraph.

"NHS claims rise lowest in 4 years"

but I do think that there should now be a Parliamentary Inquiry in to this matter.

If a public body has misled Parliament in a way that has affected the passage of legislation that affects millions of people then that is a most serious matter indeed.

NHS LITIGATION AUTHORITY: HAS IT MISLED PARLIAMENT?

"30% rise in negligence claims against NHS" screams the Daily Telegraph headline of 5 August 2011, typical of others.

No such increase ever occurred as I will demonstrate below, so where did this figure come from?

In its report to Parliament 2010-2011 the Chief Executive, Steve Walker, a Civil Servant, leaps straight in to the political arena:

"We are delighted that the Ministry of Justice is taking forward the recommendations made by Lord Justice Jackson regarding the costs of civil litigation. We believe very strongly that a regime which allows success fees and the recoverability of After-the-Event (ATE) insurance premiums makes litigation so profitable that solicitors and so-called "claims farmers" are drawn into the market thereby fuelling the rise in claims volumes we have experienced.

After large increases in previous years we saw new claims volumes for newly reported clinical claims rise by around 30% in 2010-2011 and by around 6% for non-clinical".

The truth is very different.

Conditional fee agreements were first allowed on 5 July 1995. According to the NHSLA's own figures the number of claims notified in 1997/1998, when conditional fee agreements were first becoming popular in clinical negligence claims, was 6,711. By 2009/2010 the number had fallen to 6,652.

Recoverability of success fees and ATE insurance premia came in on 1 April 2000, apparently causing the explosion in claims. Yet the 2007 NHSLA report said "the number of matters we receive has remained remarkably steady over recent years. This year there was a small decrease in the number of clinical matters in 2006/2007 over 2005/2006".

The 2008 report said: "The number of claims we receive has continued to remain remarkably steady over recent years. This year, there was an increase of less than 1% in the number of clinical claims reported".

Between 2008 and 2009 there was an increase in clinical claims of 11.30% from 5,470 to 6,088 and between 2009 and 2010 a further increase of 9.26% from 6,088 to 6,652.

The pattern of non-clinical claims very closely follows that of clinical claims, and the percentage rises in such claims between 2007-2008 and 2008-2009 was 10.74%, up from 3,380 to 3,743 and between 2008-2009 to 2009-2010 was 8.84% up from 3,743 to 4,074. Previous years show a similar close correspondence.

2010-2011

Between 2009-2010 and 2010-2011 non-clinical claims rose from 4,074 to 4,346, an increase of 6.68%.

Another measure of activity is the figure of claims open at the year end. A big surge in new claims will result in an even bigger rise in figures because it will be the older, lower, number of claims falling out whereas the new ones are all still in. On this measure non-clinical claims showed a 7.52% rise between 2009-2010 and 2010-2011 and clinical claims showed a rise of 7.51%.

So for 2010-2011 on three measures we have rises of 6.67%, 7.52% and 7.51%.

Yet clinical claims jumped from 6,652 to 8,655, an astonishing increase of 30.1%.

Very obviously this rise has nothing to do with conditional fees or recoverability of success fees and ATE as conditional fees had been in for 15 years and recoverability for 10 years, and as we have seen claims sometimes fell during the years of recoverability.

So what DOES explain it?

Nothing, because there was no such increase.

On page 12 of the report, under "Claims Received" it says:

"Formal clinical claims received under CNST [Clinical Negligence Scheme for Trusts] saw an increase of 31.6% on 2009/2010 and non-clinical claims under LTPS [Liabilities to Third Parties Scheme] rose by 7.8%. Part of the significant increase in claims under CNST may be explained to some extent by the requirement for claimants to now send us a copy of the Letter of Claim at the same time as it is sent to the defendant NHS body, at which point we now record the claim, but we are analysing patterns and trends to obtain a better understanding of the reasons behind the increase".

Thus the headline-grabbing 30% increase is pure fiction and is obviously and readily explained by a change in reporting methods.

Why did Mr Walker not mention this? Why make the politically charged, and wholly inaccurate, link between "large increases" and recoverability of success fees and After-the-Event insurance premia?

Of course next year, based on this year's higher figure and using the same, new, recording procedure the percentage increase will revert to a true figure, so it is just this one year when the percentage increase is distorted upwards.

Am I being too cynical in thinking that it suited the NHSLA to present the report to Parliament in this way this year just as Parliament is considering the abolition of recoverability?

As Disraeli said "There are lies, damned lies and statistics".

MEDICAL DEFENCE UNION: A SUITABLE CASE
FOR TREATMENT

The Medical Defence Union provides indemnity to doctors, dentists and other healthcare professionals.

In July 2014 it said that the total bill for hospital claims could cost each taxpayer at least £1,000.00 a year if inflation continues at the current pace (Law Society Gazette 18 July 2014).

As I pointed out in my blog – The NHS Lying Authority At It Again, the total cost of claims in 2013/14 was £1.244 billion, that is £20.74 per UK resident.

Based on the inflation figures for July 2014, given by the Office for National Statistics on 20 August 2014, that is 1.6%, it will take 2,967 years on a straight line basis before the annual cost reaches £1,000.00 per person, that is the year 4981.

In fact the total expenditure by the National Health Service Litigation Authority on clinical negligence and non-clinical claims *dropped* in 2013/14 as compared with 2012/13.

Dr Christine Tomkins, Chief Executive of the Medical Defence Union, referred to an award of £9 million against one surgeon in one case and said that at the current rate of inflation that will have doubled in seven years.

That is nonsense. Using the Consumer Price Index inflation figure for July 2014 of 1.6% it would take, on a straight line basis, 62 years, not seven years, for any figure to double. The actual rate over seven years will be 11.2%, not 100%.

How can someone in that position spout this rubbish? Why does the Law Society Gazette publish it without the sort of criticism that I am making here?

Extraordinarily the Medical Defence Union wants, in clinical negligence cases, a cap on the level of damages for future care costs and loss of earnings awards of three times the national average salary.

Thus a young high earner is paralysed due to clinical negligence and can never work again and needs permanent care. He or she would receive just £79,500.00 for loss of earnings for the rest of his or her life and a further

£79,500.00 for future care costs, based on the current average earnings of £26,500 a year.

In fact such future care costs run to millions of pounds.

Such a limit would be immoral. It would also not bear scrutiny under Article 6 of the European Convention on Human Rights, the right to a fair trial, and would also be an unjustified deprivation of property contrary to Article 1 of the First Protocol to the Convention.

In any event the cost of looking after such a seriously injured person, in the absence of a proper damages award, would fall upon the state anyway. So nothing would be gained.

Why does the Medical Defence Union think that its members alone, of all the people in the United Kingdom, should have the consequences of their negligence limited in this way?

Why does the Medical Defence Union think its members should be above the law?

Does the Medical Defence Union propose this for all injuries, howsoever caused? If not, why not? I wonder how a surgeon catastrophically injured in a car crash would feel getting just £79,500.00 for future care costs for the rest of his or her life and just £79,500.00 to represent maybe 30 years loss of earnings.

Organisations like the Medical Defence Union give trades unions a bad name.

This piece by my good friend Andrew Twambley first appeared in Claims Magazine Issue 21 on 1 November 2015. I am grateful to Andrew and to Claims magazine for permission to use this piece here.

HOW TO ABOLISH CLAIMS AGAINST THE NHS AND SAVE THE NATION

Andrew Twambley says the Government has again shown its true colours with its plans to abolish recoverability of ATE premiums in clinical negligence cases.

Down The Red Lion, on Parliament Street, near Downing Street, on the way home from work, Dave and George popped in for a pint of mild and a chat about how to save the nation…

Dave: Look George, we need to squirrel away some more dough. I have the bill for maintenance of my swan pond to sort out, And I can't claim it on expenses again.

George: I have a cunning stunt. We abolish the recovery of ATE premiums in clinical negligence claims against the NHS, which means we can stop the proles making claims and spending less on looking after them if they dare go into hospital.

Dave: F@@@ George, that's evil. And it will teach the poor people out there to pay up and go private – that way they will receive a 5-star service and get sorted out sooner.

George: Tee hee. They won't even be able to afford to claim. And all those blood sucking lawyers will go to the wall – meaning less people will say mean things about the ABI.

Dave: Man, this calls for a celebration. More ale barman! And make it snappy, I have swans to feed.

Dave saunters over to the jukebox and puts on the Hot Chocolate favourite, "Everyone's a Winner Baby, (and that's no lie)"

Only a couple of weeks ago I was sat next to David Pipkin of leading ATE Insurer, Temple Legal Protection, when he confirmed the rumour that the Government really want to abolish recoverability of ATE premiums in clinical negligence cases. They are already launching a "consultation" in relation to fixed fees in clinical negligence cases and intend to sneak this in by the back door, as it were!

We all know that "consultation" means the Government have already written out the new rules, but need to make it look as though they are seriously considering the views of other people.

Clinical negligence cases are risky, long winded and expensive, often because the defendants simply issue a blanket denial on the basis that they feel it will save money in the long run. If the ATE premium becomes irrecoverable, claimants will simply not be able to afford it and their lawyers will not be able to take on the additional risk.

Fewer claims will be made, and the defendants will become even more bullish with their denials.

Let us never forget that the government is often the defendant in clinical negligence cases. The plans to abolish recoverability are not objective and will not be evidence-based.

It is, at best, self-serving policy being paid for by people they have allegedly injured.

"The Party seeks power entirely for its own sake. We are not interested in the good of others; we are interested solely in power, pure power."

George Orwell, 1984

SOURCES

- The National Health Service Litigation Authority Report and Accounts 2010–2011

- The National Health Service Litigation Authority Report and Accounts 2011–2012

- The National Health Service Litigation Authority Report and Accounts 2012–2013

- The National Health Service Litigation Authority Report and Accounts 2013–2014

- The National Health Service Litigation Authority Report and Accounts 2014–2015

- The Ombudsman's Annual Report and Accounts 2013-14

- The Ombudsman's Annual Report and Accounts 2014-15

- Nuffield Foundation Funding clinical negligence cases Access to justice at reasonable cost? - Report

Section 2

Insurers at It Again

INSURERS AT IT AGAIN

The current government is in thrall to insurance companies. This influence has now become so extreme that on 25 November 2015 the Chancellor of the Exchequer, George Osborne, announced to the House of Commons in his Autumn Statement that the government would introduce legislation preventing people from recovering damages for pain suffering and loss of amenity in low value soft tissue claims.

Thus, if for example, a child is injured in a car crash caused by a drunk driver that child would not be able to claim. A policeman injured by a criminal while pursuing that criminal will not be able to claim.

However if your flight is a little late, or your train is not on time or you want to have a go at your lawyer for nothing in particular then you can still trot off to the Legal Services Ombudsman or the "My Train Was A Little Bit Late So I Want Some Dosh Ombudsman" or whatever.

This has been a cynical and prolonged campaign by insurance companies and as early as 2005 the Norwich Union suggested that there should be no damages for claims under £1,000.00 and that an apology or a bunch of flowers should suffice.

I said then – see Law Society Gazette 27 January 2005 –

"This is not the future… in fact it is going back to a situation we have not seen in this country since the early 19th century."

"What they are saying is that poor people should not be allowed access to the courts. What happens if you are injured and lose £1,000.00 wages? For a lot of people, that is a lot of money. This is basically an apartheid system for poor people."

It now looks as though all soft tissue injury claims under £5,000 will be banned.

With their massively financed and resourced publicity machine the Association of British Insurers and insurance companies generally have done a very effective job in creating a climate hostile to claimants and those injured.

One would think that there has been an explosion in claims whereas in fact the opposite is true.

The insurance companies and their representative systematically lie to anyone who will listen.

Many people realise this. What is less well-known is the extent to which they resort to despicable and illegal tactics in dealing with their insured and with third parties who are they meant to compensate and with courts and lawyers and the system generally.

Judges are not fooled by insurance companies in the way that politicians are, possibly because you cannot make huge "contributions" to judges without being locked up for a long time. The same is not true of political parties.

One day people will look back and wonder how this was ever allowed to happen. I was explaining this to a policeman in Norway and he asked why British people allowed that to happen to themselves and their fellow citizens and how was it possible to trust insurance companies as compared with your fellow citizens.

In a series of posts on my blog I have exposed these tactics and in virtually every case the information has been given to me by those in the legal profession dealing with such cases.

Unless stated otherwise these pieces have appeared as posts on my blog but not elsewhere.

I am very grateful to Andrew Twambley for his permission to include some pieces written by him on the subject for Claims Magazine, and I am also grateful to Claims Magazine.

This piece first appeared in Claims Magazine Issue 22 on 01 December 2015. I am grateful to Claims magazine for permission to use this piece here.

THE FRAUD GAME

On Wednesday 25 November 2015 the Chancellor of the Exchequer announced to the House of Commons that the small claims limit would be rising from £1,000.00 to £5,000.00, presumably in the coming financial year, that is 2016. This was presented on the basis of preventing fraud.

Now there is a proper debate to be had about the small claims limit in personal injury cases.

On the one hand in a work type where 99% of cases are won by claimants why should costs be recoverable if the damages are £1,000.00 or over as compared with £10,000.00 in breach of contract claims etc.? Indeed in the vastly more difficult, time consuming and unpredictable fields of employment law and family law there is no recoverability at all.

On the other hand the true defendants in personal injury cases are insurance companies which have the means to pay and are well organised, powerful and extremely vocal. In other words they are well able to look after themselves.

Virtually all personal injury insurance premiums are raised through compulsion; it is a criminal offence for a driver not to have motor insurance or for an employer not to have employers' liability insurance. For all intents and purposes it is a private tax. There is not necessarily anything wrong with that but it makes the issue of funding costs different from other types of law.

What I do object to is the idea that raising the small claims limit prevents fraud. It is obvious that the opposite is true.

Raising the small claims limit deters some genuine claimants and so the number of claimants, and therefore the amount of damages, drops. Unrepresented people who do bring claims will under settle, whereas lawyers rarely do.

So people are forced to pay the premiums but deterred from making a claim.

If you are the criminal type who stages or fakes an accident, how will the non-recoverability of costs put you off? You can either play the poor, hard done by "what me guv?" Litigant in Person card or treat the solicitor's contingency fee as a business expense.

Claimant lawyers reduce fraud. None want to work on a case that produces no fee income because it is lost. Even an allegation of fraud forces a claimant lawyer to do a huge amount of extra work. In a fixed costs case that extra work is for no extra fee even if the case is won.

The portal process does not apply to small claims and that process, but no other, involves the claimant solicitor in carrying out a claims history search on a client in a soft tissue matter, so as to better spot the potential fraudulent claims.

Raising the small claims limit removes that filter. It was the insurers who pushed for it. They know full well that its removal will increase fraud.

The reality is that raising the small claims limit will increase fraud in actual numbers, and because of the drop in all claims, will dramatically increase the percentage of total claims that are fraudulent.

When that happens the Association of British Insurers will tell the government to set up another fraud squad to take action against genuine claimants and so on and so on.

The ABI publicity is the true fraud in all of this.

HAVEN INSURANCE: PART ONE

Haven might mean a harbour, a shelter, a safe place but everyone in the land, as well as at sea, is well advised to give Haven Insurance a very wide berth indeed.

In the case below Haven contacted the Claimant direct and purported to do a deal specifically providing for no costs to be paid AFTER solicitors acting for the Claimant had submitted a Claim Notification Form which Haven had acknowledged in the portal.

Given the current issues before Parliament and the definition in the Qualified One-Way Costs Shifting rule you may reflect as to whether such conduct is dishonest, fundamentally dishonest, or something else.

In Kukadia v Haven Insurance Company Ltd and

Nord v Haven Insurance Company Ltd

Liverpool County Court, 20 February 2014,

District Judge Jenkinson was hearing applications by the Claimant in each case for summary judgment pursuant to CPR24.

In Kukadia the Claimant was involved in a road traffic accident on 13 December 2012 and a Claim Notification Form (CNF) was submitted on 2 January 2013 and was acknowledged by Haven the same day and liability was admitted on 7 January 2013 and on 16 January 2013 portal Stage 1 costs were paid.

However around 4 January 2013, that is after the Claimant's solicitor had lodged the CNF and after Haven had acknowledged it, Haven contacted the Claimant direct. Taking the Defendant's evidence at its highest – which is the rule in a summary judgment application – although highest may be a misnomer here – it agreed to settle the claim on the specific condition that it would not pay costs.

The District Judge decided that the issue before him was whether or not that agreement overrode paragraph 7.37 of the protocol which reads:-

"Any offer to settle made at any stage by either party will automatically include and cannot exclude:

(1)   stage 2 fixed costs in accordance with CPR 45.29;

33

(2)   an agreement in principle to pay disbursements; and

(3)   a success fee in accordance with rule 45.31(1)."

Unsurprisingly the judge found that the law as passed by Parliament was indeed the law and that the insurance company was bound by it.

It is worth reading and considering the final six paragraphs of this short Judgment as they give a flavour of the contempt shown by insurers to the law of the land, as already seen in relation to Before-the-Event insurers in my blog Insurers At It Again (1).

I set out paragraphs 9 to 14 of the Judgment in the Kukadia v Haven matter.

" 9.   It is said on behalf of the defendant, represented by Mr Whibley of counsel today, that this was an offer made outwith the protocol. Contacting the claimant directly and making such an order, Mr Whibley says, evidences the intention of the insurance company to act outside the protocol and, accordingly, to reject its provisions. He accepts and concedes they would not be able to rely upon any such offer as a proper offer within the protocol. However, it is said on behalf of the defendant, the protocol does not override the fundamental principle of freedom of contract and there is nothing that prevents the parties agreeing to settle a claim that begins its life in the protocol on terms which are inconsistent with the provisions of it.

10.   On behalf of the claimant, Mr Banks says that the provisions of 7.37 of the protocol are clear and until such time as the claim drops out of the protocol by one of the trigger factors that precipitate its leaving it, any offers automatically include and cannot exclude the offer to pay the liabilities referred to at 7.37 of the protocol. Mr Banks says that the position is quite different to Part 36, which specifically allows for offers to be made outside of Part 36 but provides that they will not have the costs protection that that particular provision of the CPR imputes. Mr Banks also says that any reference to offers pursuant to the protocol within CPR Part 36 effectively relate to a different situation, namely stage 3 offers within the protocol.

11.   The claimant brings this application for summary judgment so the claimant must establish on the basis that this application is being approached today i.e. on an interpretation of the law on the assumption that nothing would be required at a final hearing beyond the interpretation of the rules that are available now, that, on a balance of probabilities, the claimant's interpretation of the rules is correct.

12.   Against that background, I find as follows. This was a claim that was proceeding pursuant to the pre-action protocol for low value PI claims in RTA cases. The protocol is and was engaged by the provision of the claims notification form. In fact, it appears that unless the defendant performs one of the acts that specifically cause the matter to drop out of the provisions of the protocol, then it remains in the protocol for 15 days before dropping out if no response is received. However, in this case, in fact, the claimant's notification form was acknowledged by the defendant and if there was any doubt as to whether or not this matter was proceeding pursuant to the protocol, it is removed in my judgment by the admission of liability that was made, it would appear, within the portal, and the payment of stage 1 protocol costs.

13.   I proceed, therefore, on the basis that the protocol did apply. Rule 7.37 of the protocol, which I have already quoted for the purposes of this judgment, is in, in my judgment, clear and unequivocal terms. It would have been open to the drafter of the rules to add, had it been felt appropriate, "Any offer made pursuant to the protocol procedure will automatically include and cannot exclude" but that is not what rule 7.37 says. The offer was an offer that was made at a stage of the protocol because none of the triggers which removed it from the protocol had applied.

14.   Referring back to the defendant's case at its highest, the rules could have said, "Any offer made at any stage by either party will automatically include and cannot exclude," and added words "unless the parties agree otherwise." Again, that is not said. In my judgment, the logical interpretation of rule 7.37 is that *any* offer made at *any* stage by either party will *automatically* include and *cannot exclude* the responsibility to pay the additional matters set out within paragraph 7.37 of the protocol. The acceptance of the offer by the claimant means that what is automatically included by reference to paragraph 7.37 applies and in my judgment the claimant is entitled to summary judgment on the basis of the costs claimed." It is time for this sort of behaviour to be made a criminal offence under the Compensation Act and carrying a two year prison sentence. What applies to Claims Management Companies should apply to insurance companies.

To be continued

HAVEN INSURANCE: PART TWO

INSURERS, THIRD PARTY CAPTURE AND MUCH MORE: GAVIN EDMONDSON CONSIDERED

In *Gavin Edmondson Solicitors Ltd v Haven Insurance Company Ltd [2015] EWCA Civ 1230*

the Court of Appeal in allowing the solicitors' appeal, held that when an insurer is notified of a claim under the Portal and subsequently resolves the matter directly with the claimant the insurer remained liable to pay the claimant's solicitors costs under the Portal scheme.

The insurers had done this with six of Gavin Edmondson's clients. In each case they offered to pay the client more if they did not use solicitors. The insurers had adopted this as a deliberate tactic.

The solicitors had entered into Conditional Fee Agreements with the clients and used the Law Society model agreement and issued client care letters. The claims were all entered onto the road traffic Portal, that is the Protocol for Low Value Personal Injury Claims in Road Traffic Accidents.

The Court of Appeal held that equity would intervene in accordance with the case of

Khans Solicitors v Chifuntwe and another [2013] EWCA Civ 481

which established that equity will intervene to protect a solicitor's claim for fees where the paying party has notice that the receiving party's solicitor has a claim for fees.

The Court of Appeal here held that that doctrine applied when the paying party had implied notice of the outstanding fees. The immorality of the paying party's conduct was similar in each case. The court accepted that this involved an extension of the principle set out in the Khans case.

Although the solicitors' client care letter overrode the Conditional Fee Agreement and any lien which may have arisen under it, the solicitors were nevertheless entitled to recover the fixed costs and the sums payable under the Portal scheme.

The solicitors therefore had an interest which equity would protect.

The client care letter indicated that the solicitors would recover their costs from the defendant if the claim succeeded and would not charge the client anything.

The case highlights the potential problems in having terms and conditions in both a client care letter and a Conditional Fee Agreement.

The reason why here the client care letter overrode the Conditional Fee Agreement was that the client care letter contained the following paragraph:

"For the avoidance of any doubt if you win your case I will be able to recover our disbursements, basic costs and the success fee from your opponent. You are responsible for our fees and expenses only to the extent that these are recovered from the losing side. This means that if you win, you pay nothing."

The Court of Appeal accepted that there was a tension between that statement and the statement in the Conditional Fee Agreement:

"If you win your claim, you will pay our basic charges, our disbursements and success fee. The amount of fees is not based on or limited by the damages. You can claim from our opponent part or all of our basic charges, our disbursements, a success fee and insurance premium."

The Court of Appeal also proceeded on the basis that the client's waiver of entitlement to cancel the Conditional Fee Agreement within the cooling-off period was ineffective, although it is not clear as to why they formed that view, but nevertheless said that that did not relieve the insurers of their liability to pay.

The Court of Appeal said that in each case Haven, with full knowledge of the existence of Conditional Fee Agreements between the claimants and the solicitors, and full knowledge that the matters were proceeding in the Portal, made offers of settlement with no express limitation as to the period in which the offers could be accepted.

"It would have been open to Haven to make the offer conditional on cancellation of Edmondson's retainer within the permitted period, but it did not do so. In each case Haven assumed the risk that its offer might be accepted after the expiry of the cancellation period. In the event, in none of the underlying cases was the retainer cancelled or otherwise terminated."

The Court of Appeal said that the solicitors had no right to recover fees from its clients, but nevertheless in the normal course of events it did have the right to recover fixed costs under the Portal scheme.

Comment

This is one of those rare cases which deals with a number of different and important points of law. Most cases deal with only one.

Firstly it confirms the legal principle dating back to at least 1779, namely that if a paying party, knowing that a solicitor is due fees from his or her client, pays damages direct to that solicitor's client then the paying party itself must pay the opposing lawyers' fees.

This is a very important principle which few claimant personal injury lawyers understand. So often I hear complaints by claimants' lawyers that defendants are paying damages cheques direct to the claimant. That simply is not a problem as the defendants also have to pay the claimant's lawyer's fee. Thus for example if the lawyer is deducting 25% off damages of £10,000.00 the defendant pays £10,000.00 to the claimant then the defendant must also pay the lawyer's fee of £2,500.00, plus ordinary recoverable costs, as long as the defendant was on notice.

Secondly the case confirms that the indemnity principle does not apply in Portal cases, just as it does not apply in fixed recoverable costs cases – see *Butt v Nizami [2006] EWHC 159* where the court said:

"It seems to me clear that the intention underlying CPR 45.7-14 was to provide an agreed scheme of recovery which was certain and easily calculated. This was done by providing fixed levels of remuneration which might over-reward in some cases and under-reward in others, but which were regarded as fair when taken as a whole."

Thus a statement that the client will be charged nothing in any event, and a failure to make the client primarily liable for costs, which are then recoverable from the other side, does not cause a problem in Portal or fixed recoverable costs cases.

Thirdly, but related to the second point, the fact that the client was under no obligation to pay the solicitor if the Cancellation of Contracts etc Regulations had not been complied with, did not mean that the solicitor could not recover costs. This is logical. If the indemnity principle does not apply in Portal and fixed recoverable costs cases then the fact that due to a breach of the Cancellation of Contracts etc Regulations the solicitor had no right to costs from the client is irrelevant.

Thus the case *of Allpropertyclaims Ltd v Mr Tang Pang and ITC Compliance Ltd* [2015] EWHC 2198 (QB) where the court held that a breach did result in the solicitor being unable to recover costs from the other side is distinguished as in that case, not being a Portal or fixed recoverable costs case, the indemnity principle did apply.

Fourthly the court said that had the insurance company made their offers conditional on the client cancelling the contract within the period then they could have avoided paying the solicitors' costs.

I do not understand this. If the indemnity principle applies then, as per *Allpropertyclaims Ltd v Mr Tang Pang and ITC Compliance Ltd* [2015] EWHC 2198 (QB), a breach of the regulations will result in the solicitor being unable to claim costs from his or her client and therefore being unable to recover from the other side. However if the indemnity principle does not apply then the fact that the client is not liable for the costs makes no difference. In fact these cases did not involve breaches of the regulations but rather the work was done within the potential cancellation period and the client did not cancel until afterwards. The solicitors had done the work and were entitled to be paid.

Surely the same is true even if the client withdrew instructions during the cancellation period. The client had instructed the solicitors and entered into a formal Conditional Fee Agreement and received a client care letter etc. The work had been done. The fee had been earned. What the regulations do is to prevent the solicitor charging the client and normally, due to the indemnity principle, that is fatal in terms of recovering costs from the other side.

However in a Portal or fixed fee case it makes no difference – see *Butt v Nizami*.

Therefore the court's suggestion, and the comments made by many others, that all Haven need to do is change the terms of the offer to make it conditional upon the client cancelling within the cancellation period, seems to me to be wrong.

This raises a further point. Notice of cancellation does not have to be given in relation to a contract made in the solicitor's office, but most solicitors are now always giving the right to cancel within 14 days, even if the client does not have that right under the regulations. One of the reasons for this is that it is not always clear where a contract has been made. For example a client telephones and asks a solicitor if they deal with personal injury work on a No Win No Fee basis and the solicitor says yes, but we will have to see you to find out if the case is a good one.

The client then comes in and sees the solicitor who agrees to take the case. On slightly different facts, but the principle is identical, the court in *Allpropertyclaims Ltd v Mr Tang Pang and ITC Compliance Ltd* [2015] EWHC 2198 (QB) held that a contract had been made in the original conversation and it was subject to a condition precedent, namely that the solicitor thought the case had merit.

It would be a great shame if solicitors seeing clients in their office and giving them additional protection, that is the right to cancel within 14 days, were laying themselves open to an entirely opportunistic tactic by an insurance company to avoid paying solicitors for work done. All that will do is to encourage solicitors not to offer that additional protection.

Summary

This is a very welcome and a very important decision which needs to be read and understood by all claimant lawyers.

Its key point is that the court will not look favourably on insurance companies who seek to avoid paying the properly incurred legal costs of claimants. The tone of the decision suggests that the Court of Appeal is rather more aware of the reality of this country's insurance companies than is the government.

DLG LEGAL SERVICES LTD

A solicitor's client is referred to DLG Legal Services Ltd (DLG), part of the Direct Line Group (DL). It is regulated by the Solicitors Regulation Authority but from its website it seems only to accept clients who have a DL legal expenses policy. It is a firm of solicitors, not an Alternative Business Structure.

A client care letter is sent by DLG at a flat rate of £275 an hour plus VAT, whoever is dealing with the matter. I have a copy of that letter.

They are way above the rates that DL will pay to firms of solicitors instructed as the client's choice. So it pays itself getting on for double its usual rate.

Its client care letter has this odd paragraph, under "Introducers":

" This firm is appointed by Direct Line. This firm is a member of the same Group of companies as Direct Line. Aside from that your insurer has no financial interest in referring your case to us. The advice we give to you will be independent."

That is a variant on the old chestnut "Apart from that how did you enjoy the play Mrs Lincoln?"

In a free market why do not DL put the work out to firms who will happily work for a much lower rate than that?

MARKERSTUDY GROUP

A claims handler contacted a Solicitor's client direct after receipt of the Claim Notification Form showing details of the client's Solicitor.

The claims handler tells the client not to contact their own Solicitors "as this may reduce our chances of successfully investigating this matter."

It also tells the client, its opponent, that "we may take immediate steps to protect the personal data we hold about you and investigate the matter on your behalf."

Here is the text of the letter from Markerstudy Group and here is the link to the letter.

Markerstudy Group
Markerstudy Claims Department
PO Vox 726
Chesterfield
S40 9LG
Tel: 0844 973 8184
Fax: 0844 824 1666
Email: claims@markerstudy.com
WWW.MARKERSTUDY.COM

6 July 2015

Claim Number: TT15530085
Our Insured:
Date of Incident: 30 June 2015

Dear

On 2nd July 2015 we received a formal notification that you intend to claim against our policyholder for bodily injury sustained in a road traffic accident on the above date. This notification was received from the following solicitors, who claim to have received instructions from you.

[Name redacted by me]

What you need to do now

Your next course of action depends on whether or not you have instructed the solicitors named above.

a) If you have instructed the company:
if the company referred to above is known to you and you have provided them with formal instructions to pursue a claim on your behalf, we simply ask that you contact us with confirmation. You can do this by one of the following methods:
1) Call us on **01245 254091**
2) E-mail us at **PIClaims@markerstudy.com**
3) Write to us at **PO Box 726, Chesterfield, S40 9LG**
Please quote our reference number when contacting us.
Following confirmation from you, all further communication regarding your claim will be directed to the solicitors and you will receive no further contact from us directly.

b) If you have NOT instructed the company:
if you have no knowledge of the company referred to above and/or you have not issued them with any formal instructions to pursue a claim on your behalf please contact us immediately by calling **01245 254091** or by e-mailing us at **PIClaims@markerstudy.com** so that we can take immediate steps to protect the personal data we hold about you and investigate the matter on your behalf.

To assist with investigations please include a telephone number, to enable us to contact you to obtain any further information required.

Please rest assured any communication with you will be treated in the strictest confidence. Please do not contact the company referred to above as this may reduce our chances of successfully investigating this matter.

General Information

As part of the claims process we will register your personal details with the Department of Works Pensions (DWP) Compensation Recovery Unit; this being a statutory requirement. The DWP works with Insurers to recover benefits arising out of insurance claims.

Markerstudy passes claim information to the Claims and Underwriting Exchange register (administered by IDC Ltd), MIAFTR (administered by the ABI) and other databases in order to assist with the prevention and detection of fraud. We will also search these and other databases, as well as share claims data with other insurers and organisations for the same purposes.

Yours sincerely

Claims Department.

MINSTER LAW

A client reports a matter to Aviva. Without her knowledge the information is sent to Minster Law who submit a Claim Notification Form (CNF) on the portal.

Two days after the accident her actual solicitors, who are unaware of this, submit CNFs for her and for the driver of the car. The client's CNF is rejected as a duplicate.

The solicitors telephone and write several times to the third party insurer and eventually they ask the solicitors to resubmit the CNF, which they do, only for that also to be rejected.

Consequently the solicitors issue proceedings and the matter proceeds to a disposal hearing.

Costs were not assessed on the day as the defendant alleged unreasonable removal from the portal, a point repeated in the Points of Dispute during provisional assessment.

The matter is listed for an oral hearing. The day before that hearing solicitors for the defendant insurers concede the point and agree to pay the costs of the main case and of detailed assessment.

EVER SEEN WORSE TH>N MORE TH>N?

Below is the text of a letter sent by MORE TH>N, a trading name of Royal & Sun Alliance Insurance plc, to a solicitor's client questioning whether the client had actually instructed those solicitors at all. That appears to be an actionable libel, but let that pass.

The letter then assumes that the client has indeed instructed the solicitors. It asks the client to confirm that fact and writes to this client of a firm of solicitors *on the other side*:-
"When responding we would also ask that you confirm how you came to instruct the firm in question?" [sic]
"Did someone else refer you to them?
Did they contact you direct?

Did you contact them direct?"

Towards the end the letter says:-

"Deliberately fabricating losses, or exaggerating the value of your losses, is an offence under the Fraud Act 2006."

Imagine a solicitor writing that to a lay client *on the other side who has already instructed solicitors*. That would be getting into striking off territory. It is potentially contempt of court to seek to dissuade another solicitor's client direct from pursuing a claim by what could be construed as a threat, where those solicitors have initiated a claim through the court process, which lodging a CNF clearly is.
It gets worse.

The client telephoned MORE TH>N and was offered £1,500.00 direct and told that her solicitor, Infinity Law Ltd T/A DGM Solicitors as in the letter, would charge her more and she would come out with hardly anything.

They also told her that she had 14 days to cancel and so her solicitors could not charge her anything.

Thus a client protection measure – the right to cancel – becomes a way of the *other side,* seeking to prevent the client having legal representation. That is obviously very harmful to the client and causes far more damage than not having the right to cancel in the first place. The other side here is a massive insurance company.
The writer of this letter, without irony, is described as a "Customer Services Director".

46

Here is a link to the actual <u>Letter</u>, the text of which is set out below.

MORE TH>N

Claims Department

PO Box 21561

STIRLING

FK7 1AA

T   0330 1023630

F   01403 325889

E   claims@morethan.com

07 August 2015

Claim Number:

Our Insured:

Date of Accident:

Dear Mr

We have received a personal injury claims notification form from Infinity Law Ltd T/A DGM Solicitors, advising that that you have asked them to make a claim for injury on your behalf following a road traffic accident on the above date.

In the interests of preventing fraud, which has been on the increase, we hope you will not mind us writing directly to you in order to confirm that you are aware that Infinity Law Ltd T/A DGM Solicitors have made a claim on your behalf alleging you have suffered whiplash as a result of the above accident.

What to do Next
This depends on whether or not you have asked Infinity Law Ltd T/A DGM Solicitors to make a claim for these injuries on your behalf.

If you have asked the solicitors to make a claim on your behalf:
If you did ask these Solicitors to make a personal injury claim on your behalf, then we would be grateful if you could please confirm this to us. When responding we would also ask that you confirm how you came to instruct the firm in question? Did someone refer you to them? Did they contact you direct? Did you contact them direct?

After we hear from you, we will; not contact you again directly, and will deal exclusively with your solicitors.

Please contact us using any of the following methods quoting reference:

Email at:

Telephone on number 01422325255

Post Po Box 256 Wymond, NR18 9DQ

If you have not asked the solicitors to make a personal injury claim on your behalf:
If you have not asked Infinity Law Ltd T/A DGM Solicitors to make a claim for injury against our policyholder please contact us without delay by calling this dedicated number 01422325536 or by e-mailing us at alexandra.z.greaves@uk.rsagroup.com. We will take immediate steps to protect the position of your personal data and will also look into this matter further on your behalf.

If you do not want to pursue a personal injury claim, but have been told by an agency or other party that you will be charged a fee, please telephone us on 01422325536 and we will be happy to offer you further assistance.

It would be helpful if when writing you provide a telephone number in order that we can contact you to discuss this matter further.

Please be assured that any communication will be dealt with in confidence.

General Information for all Claimants:
Like most people we are sure that you will agree that exaggerating or making up claims against insurers is wrong, it cause motor insurance premiums to increase, and puts genuine victims of accidents in a bad light. We thank you for your assistance in helping us and the insurance industry as whole combat fraudulent claims.

As part of the claims process, we are obliged by law to register your personal details with the Department for Work and Pensions (DWP) Compensation Recovery Unit. The DWP works with insurers to recover benefits arising out of insurance claims.

We also pass claims information to the Claims and Underwriting Exchange (CUE), MIAFTR and other databases in order to assist with the prevention and detection of fraud. We may also search these and other databases, as well as share claims data with other insurers and organisations for the same purpose.

Deliberately fabricating losses, or exaggerating the value of your losses, is an offence under the Fraud Act 2006.

Thank you for your attention and assistance.

Yours sincerely

_____

Customer Service Director

DIRECT LINE OR DIRECT LYING?

In a previous piece I commented on Direct Line Group and its relationship with DLG Legal Services, a firm of solicitors and part of the Direct Line Group.

The standard client care letter from that firm to its "clients" states "This firm is appointed by Direct Line."

Clients – for which read insured of Direct Line – are not asked to sign anything but are rather told:-

"This letter and the attached Terms of Business set out the contract between us, and unless we hear from you to the contrary we will assume that you are happy for us to act based on the terms of the policy of insurance in place with your insurers."

So what you may think. Well how about this, at paragraph 14 of the Terms of Business, which the client is not asked to sign:-

"14. Limitation of Liability
Your relationship is solely with DLG Legal Services. We have sole legal liability for the work done for you. No director or member of staff working as an employee or in any other capacity at DLG Legal Services will have legal liability for that work whether in contract, tort, or on any other basis. Our liability to you for a breach of your instructions shall be limited to 200% of the amount of our fees for the matter or £100,000.00, whichever is the lesser, unless we expressly state a higher amount in the letter accompanying these Terms and Conditions of Business. We will not be liable for any consequential, special, indirect or exemplary damages, costs or losses, or any damages, costs or losses attributable to lost profits or opportunities. We can only limit our liability to the extent the law allows. In particular, we cannot limit our liability for death or personal injury caused by our negligence. Please ask if you would like us to explain any of the terms above."

Let us say that firm settles a matter in the portal and receives a portal fee of £500.00. The client sues as it turns out that the claim may be worth £20,000.00 or whatever more than it was actually settled for.

This firm of solicitors, independent of, but "appointed by" – their words – Direct Line are seeking to limit their professional indemnity liability to £1,000.00 in a claim settled in the portal.

I wonder what view the Solicitors Regulation Authority would take of any of the rest of us who sought to do that:-

"Sorry, we screwed up on your conveyancing and you have lost £1 million, but we only charged you £400.00 so here is our cheque for £800.00."

Why does my firm have to have minimum Professional Indemnity Insurance of £3 million if we are free to limit our liability to just twice our costs on any particular matter?

In 2012 the Financial Services Authority fined Direct Line and Churchill Insurance £2 million because 27 out 50 files requested by the Financial Services Authority for review were "altered improperly" before they were submitted to the Financial Services Authority and seven internal documents were found to contain signatures that had been forged – see Daily Mail 19 January 2012
At the time Direct Line was owned by the Royal Bank of Scotland. It no longer is. One year earlier the Royal Bank of Scotland was fined £2.8 million for "multiple failings" in complaints handling.

As at August 2015 the Government of the United Kingdom held and managed a 73% stake in the Royal Bank of Scotland through UK Financial Investments.

Imagine the consequences for any of the rest of us of altering improperly 27 out of 50 files requested by the Solicitors Regulation Authority and forging signatures. Why is Direct Line Group allowed to have any formal connection with a firm of solicitors?

UK Assistance
There is a company called UK Assistance, also part of Direct Line Insurance Group Plc and with the same registered office, and the "appointers" of DLG Legal Services, a firm of solicitors regulated – or perhaps not – by the Solicitors Regulation Authority.

Attached is a letter from UK Assistance to a client of a different firm of solicitors where a Claim Notification Form had already been submitted on the portal on that client's behalf by that firm. Note the email contact details. The text reads:-

Dear Mr

Road traffic accident on:
I have been instructed by Insurance Company, Peugeot, to contact you regarding this incident. A claim has been submitted in your name for personal injuries and we are required to check the details of the claim submitted before being in a position to proceed further.

UK Assistance provides specialist services to insurers, to assist them with their enquiries into incidents of this type.

Peugeot Insurance has requested that I arrange to meet you to discuss this incident in more detail. I would be grateful if you could telephone me on 07967 650 575 or email me at melony.buchan@directlinegroup.co.ukas soon as possible, in order to arrange an appointment.
I shall look forward to hearing from you.

Yours sincerely

[Name redacted by me]

CLAIMS INSPECTOR

UK Assistance then sent an investigator to the client's home in the full knowledge that the client had already instructed solicitors to pursue a claim.

How ironic that governments of all parties have abolished legal aid and yet have poured billions of pounds into failed banks to allow them to act in this way against the ordinary decent people of this country who have to pay their taxes to bail out these failed multinational institutions.

Many of you may have a term stronger than ironic in mind.

DLG LEGAL SERVICES & SOLICITORS CODE OF CONDUCT

Following publication of this blog several people, including Richard Moorhead and my own business partner Robert Males have pointed out that this appears to be a breach of the Solicitors Code of Conduct.

Outcome 1.8 of the Code of Conduct states that clients have the benefit of compulsory professional indemnity insurance "and you do not exclude or attempt to exclude liability below the minimum level of cover required by the SRA Indemnity Insurance Rules 2013 which require a minimum cover of £2 million for a partnership or £3 million for an incorporated firm."

Outcomes are compulsory and are designed to achieve the principles which in this case would be:-

- Act with integrity
- Act in the best interest of each client
- Behave in a way that maintains the trust the public places in you and in the provision of legal services.

I am not holding my breath that the Solicitors Regulation Authority will take any action. Of course if it was any ordinary firm of solicitors they would be down on us like a ton of bricks.

This piece first appeared in Claims Magazine Issue 11 on 01 January 2014. I am grateful to Claims magazine for permission to use this piece here.

FRAUD AND RTA: NEW GUIDANCE

Kerry Underwood provides a tongue-in-cheek update on the insurance industry's monitoring of fraud

Ash for Cash	Artificial volcanoes are erupted to cause ash cloud and accidents and claims.
Bash for Cash	Still the most popular scam; motorists have genuine accidents and claim on the insurance that they have paid for. Some consider this not to be true fraud; others think that any genuine claim must at least be fundamentally dishonest.
Cash for Cash	Banks. The biggest fraud of all.
Dash for Cash	Olympic runners take part in an apparently spontaneous 100 metres race on a motorway, causing crashes and claims.
Fash for Cash	Models stage fashion shows on roads, with the inevitable outcome.
Flash for Cash	Models take their clothes off – see Fash for Cash.
Lash for Cash	A public whipping is staged on a main road. Not to be confused with whiplash.
Mash for Cash	Mashed potato is spread on the road.
Rash for Cash	Children with spots painted on their faces appear in the road, causing concerned motorists to brake.
Slash for Cash	Self-explanatory.
Splash for Cash	See Slash for Cash.
Tash for Cash	Fraudsters stop cars and offer to paint moustaches on the occupants, thus causing accidents.
Trash for Cash	Public Relations department of an insurance company.
Wash for Cash	Doesn't rhyme except in the North-East.
Whiplash for Cash	An unpleasant and painful injury and therefore not at all fraudulent, but it suits insurance companies and the Constitutional Lord Justice Ministry of Chancellors Affairs Department and Truth and similarly honest bodies to lump it in with genuine fraud.

The Association of British Fraudsters has issued guidance and a glossary concerning fraud and road traffic accidents. The aim is to create accidents so that a claim may be made.

Right to lawyer in BTE cases
Meanwhile, in other insurance-related news, the European Court of Justice has ruled that legal expenses insurers must allow insured people to choose freely a lawyer or suitably qualified legal representative, rather than forcing people to have the matter dealt with inhouse by DAS employees.

In *DAS Nederlandse Rechtsbijstand Verzekeringsmaatschappij NV*, 7 November 2013 the ECJ held that Article 4(1)(a) of Council Directive 87/344/EEC of 22 July 1987 prevents legal expense insurers from insisting that the matter will be dealt with by its own employees, even if that is stipulated in the contract of insurance.

This is the case whether or not legal assistance is compulsory under national law in the inquiry or proceedings concerned.

This is the second such ruling against DAS following the decision in *(1) Brown – Quinn (2) Webster Dixon LLP v (1) Equity Syndicate Management Ltd and (2) Motorplus Ltd [2012] EWCA1633* that insured people had the right to choose their own lawyer.

In the new case DAS accepted that, but argued that its insured had no right to a lawyer at all under the terms of the policy and that DAS could insist on it being dealt with in-house.
That argument was comprehensively rejected by the European Court of Justice. DAS is dat then!

FREEDOM OF CHOICE OF SOLICITORS

Wonga and the Student Loans Company (SLC) have demonstrated once again that many financial institutions in this country feel free to break the law with impunity, and apparently, immunity. Before-the-Event insurers are amongst the worst offenders and nothing has been done in spite of scathing criticisms by the courts.

Recently NatWest (Home Legal Expenses Department) wrote to a firm of solicitors as follows:

'The issue regarding freedom of choice of solicitor has been debated for some time now and the Financial Ombudsman Service (FOS) has provided guidance to the industry on this point. In line with this guidance we will allow freedom of choice of solicitor only on claims with complex legal issues, or where there is a considerable history, or high value. Any decision we make regarding legal representation is made with these guidance points in mind, where we consider that the FOS would support our position.

From the information provided to us regarding our policyholder's claim, we do not consider their case to be one where we would be expected to allow freedom of choice. We therefore would not be willing to agree to your appointment and would insist on appointing one of our nominated solicitors to act for our policyholder up to the point of issue of proceedings.'

The Financial Ombudsman Service's website, wrongly, states:

'Legal expenses policies often give the insurer the freedom to choose which solicitors to appoint for advice and assistance up to the time where legal proceedings start – unless there is a conflict of interest.

However, once proceedings start (when the legal "claim form" is issued) – or if there is a conflict of interest – the law (regulation 6 of the Insurance Companies (Legal Expenses Insurance) Regulations 1990 [SI 1159]) allows policyholders to choose their own solicitors.

These regulations are wide enough to include legal proceedings pursued and defended in tribunals – for example, employment tribunals – as well as proceedings in courts.

Insurers usually have panel solicitors whom they regularly instruct. We sometimes see disputes where a policyholder wants to appoint their own solicitor from the start (or have already instructed their own solicitor prior to making the claim).

Insurers sometimes have no objection to using a policyholder's own solicitor. But for legitimate commercial and quality-control reasons, insurers often prefer to use their solicitors from their own panel.

We look at each case on its own individual merits. However, we are likely to decide that the policyholder should be able to appoint their own solicitors from the start only in exceptional circumstances.'

The law is very different and I set it out here:

In *Jan Sneller v DAS Nederlandse Rechtsbijstand Verzekeringsmaatschappij NV*, European Court of Justice, 7 November 2013
DAS, the before-the-event legal expenses insurer involved, stated that it was only prepared to provide legal assistance to Mr Sneller through one of its own unqualified members of staff, rather than through a qualified lawyer chosen by Mr Sneller.

The Supreme Court of the Netherlands referred the following question to the European Court of Justice:

"Does Article 4(1) of Directive [87/344] allow a legal expenses insurer, which stipulates in its policies that legal assistance in inquiries or proceedings will in principle be provided by employees of the insurer, also to stipulate that the costs of legal assistance provided by a lawyer or legal representative freely chosen by the insured person will be covered only if the insurer takes the view that the handling of the case must be subcontracted to an external lawyer?"

The answer is no. Thus the insured person must have the freedom to choose his own lawyer or other person appropriately qualified under national law, although in certain cases limitations may be imposed by the insurer on the level of costs.

In *(1) Brown – Quinn (2) Webster Dixon LLP v (1) Equity Syndicate Management Ltd and (2) Motorplus Ltd* [2012] EWCA1633
the Court of Appeal examined in detail the law concerning the right to choose one's own lawyer under a legal expenses policy.

Article 4 of Council Directive 87/344 EEC provides:

"1. Any contract of legal expenses insurance shall expressly recognise that:

a) where recourse is had to a lawyer or other person appropriately qualified according to national law in order to defend, represent or serve the interests

57

of the insured person in any inquiry or proceedings, that insured person shall be free to choose such lawyer or other person.

b) the insured person shall be free to choose a lawyer or, if he so prefers to the extent that national law so permits, any other appropriately qualified person, to serve his interests whenever a conflict of interests arises.

205 provide for legal expenses insurance in the same terms. The 1987 Directive was transposed into English Law by the Insurance Companies (Legal Expenses Insurance) Regulations 1990 and the equivalent of the old Article 4 is Regulation 6 which provides:

"Freedom to choose lawyer

6

(1) Where under a legal expenses insurance contract recourse is had to a lawyer (or other person having such qualifications as may be necessary) to defend, represent or serve the interests of the insured in any inquiry or proceedings, the insured shall be free to choose that lawyer (or other person).

(2) The insured shall also be free to choose a lawyer (or other person having such qualifications as may be necessary) to serve his interests whenever a conflict of interests arises.

(3) The above rights shall be expressly recognised in the policy."

The insurers operated a system of panel solicitors whereby solicitors agreed to charge either a fixed hourly rate or a total fixed fee irrespective of the importance or complexity of the work or of the experience or qualifications of the person carrying out the work.

The insurers also had a system of standard terms of appointment for non-panel solicitors providing for hourly rates of between £125 and £139. If an insured person wished to appoint a non-panel solicitor then the insurer would only agree to that appointment and be responsible for the fees if the solicitor agreed to the standard terms of appointment, including those hourly rates.

The non-panel solicitors sought a declaration that the insurers were bound to pay their fees at their hourly rate up to the limit of the insurance.

In two conjoined cases the clients wished to move from the panel solicitors to the same firm of non-panel solicitors, Messrs Webster Dixon, but the insurers refused to pay them anything and they sought a declaration that the insurers were bound to continue to support their cases. The solicitor at Webster Dixon had dealt with the cases all along as he had moved from the panel firm originally dealing with them.

At first instance the High Court held that the non-panel rates were relevant as a comparator, but not as a starting point and that any assessment should take in to account the availability of other suitable firms of solicitors charging less than Webster Dixon and that the following should also be taken into account:

(a) the location of the chosen solicitors compared to the panel solicitors;

(b) their specialisation and qualification for taking on the claim;

(c) the complexity of the claims;

(d) the importance of the claim to the client;

(e) the substance and strength of the proposed defendant to the claims; and

(f) the nature of the work to be carried out, e.g. whether it was appropriate to be conducted by a senior solicitor or partner of the firm.

Such an assessment would be neither an ordinary assessment taking account of those matters relevant to costs under the Civil Procedure Rules, nor an assessment adopting the non-panel rates as a starting point.

The judge held that a claimant who reasonably instructed a non-panel solicitor in the middle of a case was in the same position as a claimant who instructed such a solicitor from the outset.

The Court of Appeal set aside the High Court order and granted a declaration that the defendants were bound to pay the non-panel rates, but no more.

Thus the law is that a client has freedom of choice of solicitor, but will only recover the non-panel rates determined by the insurer.

Thus the non-panel solicitor must either settle for those rates or charge the insured client the extra, that is the difference between the non-panel rate and their actual charging rate. This can easily be achieved by a no win lower fee conditional fee agreement – see *Gloucestershire County Council v Evans [2008] EWCA Civ 21*.
The Court of Appeal based its decision on Paragraph 33 of the judgement of the European Court of Justice in

Stark v DAS Oesterreichische Allgemeine Rechtsschutz – Versichergung A.G (2011)
Case c-293/10,
which reads:

" 33. Consequently, freedom of choice, within the terms of Article 4(1) of Directive 87/344, does not mean that Member States are obliged to require insurers, in all circumstances, to cover in full the costs incurred in connection with the defence of an insured person, irrespective of the place where the person professionally entitled to represent that person is established in relation to the court or administrative authority with jurisdiction to deal with a dispute, on condition that that freedom is not rendered meaningless. That would be the case if the restriction imposed on the payment of those costs were to render de facto impossible a reasonable choice of representation by the insured person. In any event, it is for national courts … to determine whether or not there is any such restriction."

The Court of Appeal held that there was no evidence that the rates offered were so insufficient as to render the insured's freedom of choice meaningless. The Guideline Rates for Summary Assessment were of no relevance.

The Court of Appeal took the opportunity to launch a savage attack on the before-the-event insurers involved stating (paragraph 8)

"The facts of this case have revealed that the insurers exhibit an insouciance to their obligations under the Directive and the Regulations which leaves one quite breathless". The Regulations (and the Directive) make it entirely clear that the insured's freedom to have the lawyer of his choice is to be expressly stated in the contract made with the insured. What the contracts in the present case provide in General Condition 2.3 is almost the opposite…"

At Paragraph 13 the Court of Appeal said:

"It is very difficult to view all this conduct as the conduct of a reasonable and responsible insurers…" and that it viewed the insurer's behaviour with "distaste".

And finally at Paragraph 33

"It is quite wrong that, despite the warning shot delivered to legal expenses insurers by this court in Sarwar v Alam [2002] 1 WLR 125 para 44, insurers should many years later be issuing policies which do not comply with the Regulations, General Conditions 2.3 and 5 are in breach of the Regulations in the ways I have explained and must be either deleted or comprehensively re-drafted."

[Regulation 5 provided, illegally,

"If an appointed representative refuses to continue acting for you or if you dismiss an appointed representative, the cover we provide will end at once, unless we agree to appoint another appointed representative."

Regulation 2.3 provided, illegally,

"If we agree to start legal proceedings and it becomes mandatory for you to be represented by a lawyer, or there is a conflict of interest, you can choose an appointed representative by sending us the suitably qualified person's name and address. We may choose not to accept the choice of representative, but only in exceptional circumstances. If there is a disagreement over the choice of appointed representative, another suitably qualified person can be appointed to decide the matter. Before you choose a lawyer, we can appoint an appointed representative."]

It is time all Ombudsmen were abolished. They are a waste of space, woefully ignorant and very expensive and are harming this country and the rule of law.

It is also time that insurers who deliberately lie and draft illegal policies are prosecuted for contempt of court. Imprisoning a few directors of Before-the-Event insurers for a couple of weeks will end the practice.

The remaining pieces in this section are by Andrew Twambley and first appeared in Claims Magazine and I am grateful to them both for allowing me to reproduce them here.

GREEDY BASTARD CLAIMANTS

Andrew Twambley imagines a future with no claimants

So 2013 has begun and claimants and their lawyers can look forward to an uncertain future with perhaps fewer lawyers and claimants being bullied into accepting paltry settlements. Well at least there is some good news, insurance premiums will come down as promised by those charitable magnanimous insurers.

But no… I read *The Daily Lie* in disbelief. Despite the insurance companies achieving more success than General Montgomery in the African desert, it looks like premiums are about to soar. This is not due to naughty accident management companies, success fees, greedy lawyers (all deceased) or 'cash for crash' scandals, it is because people who are injured are receiving pay outs from insurers via the courts. How shocking is this? To quote one respected daily paper (5.1.13),

"Drivers face paying hundreds of pounds more a year for their insurance due to soaring compensation awards made by the courts. As well as giving lump sums, to claimants with life chancing injuries such as brain damage, courts are now making periodic payment orders to cover their ongoing care."

For God's sake, how dare these, greedy, paralysed people with life-changing injuries make claims in order to "allegedly" put their lives back together? They are obviously making all this up and exaggerating. They are the root cause of the compensation culture.

In fact, they must be the reason the whole country is in such a mess – or so my Uncle Jack tells me. Thanks to the ABI for pointing this out to the press. People having serious injuries must be a new thing because that's why premiums are once again going up and not down, as the insurers promised.

And what's this about periodic payments? What a scam. These injured people should wait until the end of the case, until they have lost.

Anyway, why should the insurers pay out to these seriously injured people in any event> Most claims are obviously fraudulent and those who do suffer such injuries are probably to blame anyway. So why should they receive compensation?

"If I was in power I would change the law to say that there should be no pay-outs. Then insurers would have more money to give to the government to run their re-election campaigns and everyone would be a winner. And we would get rid of all the fat cat lawyers, double bonus. By the time I am grown up, that will already have been done."

Arthur Elwen Cameron aged 8 and a quarter

AFTERNOON TEA AT NO. 10 (A WINTER'S PLAY)
A short play by Andrew Twambley

The scene

The library at No. 10 Downing Street. A fire is roaring and the lighting is dimmed. *Moonlight Sonata by Beethoven* is playing in the background on an old record player.

Cast of characters

David Cameron: PM, ex-Bullingdon Boy and Vote Buyer

Failing Grayling: Supposed Justice Minister who has never held down a real job

Larry The Cat: The real powerhouse in Downing Street (mouse catcher)

The setting

The scene opens with David Cameron sitting on his throne wearing a gold lame smoking jacket. Larry is on his lap. There is a knock at the door.

DC: Enter subject and state your purpose

The door opens and in comes Failing Grayling bowing and looking at the floor.

FG: Good day, Your Majesty, how may I serve you best today (*he is sweating and looks apprehensive*)

DC: Ah Grayling, I have been looking at your recent performance and am not impressed to say the least. You seem to be... looking after the people!

FG: But... but... Master, I am only acting at your behest.

DC: You are supposed to be sucking up to the big insurers and making sure they contribute millions to our otherwise doomed election campaign. BUT, I see you have failed to raise the Small Claims Limit and done another U-turn, this time on that messo... meeso, miso..... lungy portal thing. The insurers are well mad! You going soft on me?

FG: No Your Worship, there was absolutely no credible evidence in favour of raising the small claims limit and the lungy thing, well, that was so against the interests of those suffering, I…

DC stands, is frothing at the mouth and turning purple. Larry is thrown to the floor.

DC: (*shouting*) When, has that had any bearing on how we act? Do you not like your moat, your duck-house and your newly refurbished Osborne and Little designed office suite?

FG: (*falling at DC's feet*) But, My Leader…..

DC: Don't but but me, you little bald slime, go and issue a statement that small claims is NOT off the agenda and them wheezers are going to be treated like all the other proles out there. We need funds. End of.

FG (*cowering*): Yes, oh magnificent One, I will get right on it…

DC: And one last thing. Imagine you're at The Job Centre. What are you qualified to do? What real experience do you have, apart from licking off your golden spoon? Now get out!

FG (*Walking backwards bending at the waist*) Yes Master.

FG leaves the room, DC sits back down, Larry jumps back on DC's lap.

Larry: Who the @@@@ was that worm?

DC: Don't ask. Some maggot I put in charge of the Justice System, to ensure we receive a huge wad in time for the next election.

Larry sees a mouse and pounces off DC's lap.

Lights darken to rapturous applause…

DIRTY DEALINGS IN THE CITY

Andrew Twambley *presents the continuing chronicles of George and Dave*

Picture the scene. It's 2 p.m. on Wednesday 24 November in The Slug and Sausage, on St Mary Axe, just below the HQ of one of our huge trusted insurance companies. Dave and George sit in a corner huddled over their second bottle of Dom Perignon, discussing the morning's meeting and the following day's Autumn Statement.

Dave: Hey G, pass us another one of those pickled swan's eggs. Now what's this about tomorrow's spending review you want to discuss?

George: If we want to continue to receive the huge donations from our insurer partners, they have made it quite plain that we need to do more to boost their indecent profits. So I have come up with a plan.

Dave: Go on G, what is it? Appoint Donald Trump Secretary of State for Justice?

George: *(Ignoring Dave's sarcasm)* I am going to raise the small claims limit for injuries to £5K and disallow damages sustained in minor RTAs and will say it is to tackle fraud!

Dave: @$*% George, it's supposed to be a spending review. Claims don't cost us a penny as it's just money going round in circles. Where has this brainwave come from?

George: Well, them upstairs say it needs to happen or millions of pounds of 'donations' to the party, may, well, dry up. And, let us not forget, all the gifts they buy in order to help me balance the books. Why, it costs me £40 billion per year just to pay the interest on the national debt. Without their investment, we would be up poo creek.

Dave: Jeez G, this sounds like a conversation at FIFA! Surely it was only two years ago that we sent off the Transport Select Committee to report on this when they firmly said NO to the £5K?

George: What do they know?

Dave: But George Old Boy, that would mean the majority of people injured due to someone else's negligence will be unable to obtain legal assistance. If they do claim they will be up against multi-national insurers with bucketloads of lawyers and tons of cash. That will be unfair, potentially.

George: Dave. Look at me. Do I look bovered? Look, it will be fair coz I will set up a consultation (wink wink), which I will obviously ignore, and I will get Govey to sort out an impact assessment based on the figures that the boffins at the ABI produce. And hey presto!!

Dave: I like it. But have you actually thought about the cost to the country?

George: Such as?

Dave: Well, off the top of me head, there's loss of court fees, loss of consumer spending in the economy, loss of CRU contributions, more litigants-in-person clogging up the courts (in those that stay open), a resurgence of unregulated CMCs, and my legacy as "the man who destroyed the justice system". Plus I know we hate lawyers, but there will be hundreds of thousands more on unemployment benefits to fork out. And we lose their income tax.

George: (*with his fingers in his ears*) Na na na na na, Na na na na na. I am not listening!

Dave: Georgie, be serious

George: Look Dave, I am deadly serious, now let's get back to Downing Street, I can prepare the speech and you can plan some air strikes on more innocent civilians. Taxi!

Section 3

Dick Chilblain

Miscellaneous off the wall pieces

Dick Chilblain

Dick Chilblain is an amalgam of a few legal journalists who appear to think that the only news worth reporting is that of unqualified people trying to break into the law – something which they have tried to do unsuccessfully for the past 1,000 years.

As the failure of the Legal Services Act 2007 and Alternative Business Structures becomes more apparent each day, and as evidence of the great harm that they are doing to society emerges, so the ramblings of these apologists become ever more extreme.

Dick Chilblain started as a parody of such journalists but the real journalists' musings about Alternative Business Structures are such that they have become a parody of Dick Chilblain.

I hasten to add that the vast majority of legal journalists are talented, know their stuff and understand the importance to society of the rule of law and lawyers, while not being blind to the shortcomings of the system, particularly in relation to costs.

All of these pieces have appeared only as posts on my blog.

ELVIS: THE ABS

A Dick Chilblain Special!

As Elvismania grips Hertfordshire ahead of the King's appearance at Bovingdon Cricket Club this Saturday Ace Reporter Dick Chilblain dropped in to Heartbreak Hotel, the HQ of the new Elvis Alternative Business Structure, where all advice is sung using the titles of Elvis songs.

Dick arrived as Penny Lane, a solicitor with an identity problem, re-capped her client's position:

So, Long Tall Sally Quindell-Stobart you met Danny at A Little Cabin on the Hill. He asked Are You Lonesome Tonight; you said I Want You, I Need You, I Love You and there followed a Hawaiian Wedding Song.

That's When Your Heartaches Began. Marie's the Name of His Latest Flame. There was Trouble. You were All Shook Up and said "You're A Heartbreaker." Now you have only Memories and you want Money Honey.

LTSQ-S: Yes, that's right. Why are you singing and curling your lip?

PL: That's what we do here. Is it So Strange?

Next door Penny Lane's colleague is seeing Danny. Fearless Dick Chilblain asked about Ethics:

"Yes, we will be opening an office there soon."

So, Danny, Marie's the Name of your Little Sister. This is about Suspicious Minds. You don't want to go your Separate Ways. Long Tall Sally is Always on Your Mind. You want to Patch it Up.

DQ-S:Yes, why are you singing and wearing a gold suit?

Trust me – I am an Alternative Business Structure.

Mr Justice Moneybags of Singapore cut short his dream of publicly caning a few people to say that lawyers had to cut fees, and if needs be records and anything else, and this was a welcome move to keep whichever country he was now a judge in at the forefront of international commercial arbiration.

NEXT WEEK: Dick Chilblain visits the Upside Down Dentist Alternative Tooth Structure.

ABS Past would like to acknowledge the role of Mr Andrew Twambley in suggesting the idea of an Elvis ABS.

UPSIDE DOWN DENTISTS

Another Dick Chilblain exclusive!

An innovative Alternative Tooth Structure plans to dominate the market and open 2953 shops in 34.7 days by having dentists work on conshoomers teeth whilst upside down. The business has an IOU for the standard 12 million required to dominate any market, although these appear to be Colombian pesos worth £3,120 arising from the import of cocaine for the new business.

Nigel Neutron, 94, nuclear weapons tester (retired) explained:-

"I've got my pension but no teeth left and that got me thinking about what would get me to pay for a dentist now that I have not got any teeth. It would have to be something new and different and exciting!"

Nigel discussed the benefits:-

"The dominant dentist compliant patient role is reversed. No one can respect an upside down dentist, so the fear is removed. The idea of a trained and qualified dentist standing over a patient is frankly very 20th century."

Due to the demands of hanging upside down the work will in fact be performed by monkeys.

"Children love it" explained Neutron – "instead of being told that they are going to the dentist their parents, if I can use such an old fashioned term, tell them that "the monkey is going to play with you."

Unfortunately Oswald the Orangutang did just that and is now on the Primate Sex Offenders Register, "but that's happened with non-upside down dentists as well" says Neutron.

Asked if he had any plans to take the idea to other professions, such as the law, Neutron was dismissive:-

"That is stupid. Law needs intelligent, learned people; it is not a physical thing like dentistry. No, I can never see the day when law could be practised by non-lawyers filling in as lawyers. That is a bridge too far."

NEXT WEEK: How to start your own heart transplant business.

Here are comments and replies on this blog page.

Starting your own Heart Transplant business is all well and good, but how does that help me? You see I have eaten a tad too much and enjoyed a few splashes of Rioja above the relevant quota. I think a new heart would do nicely.

But I probably can't afford to pay for a surgeon and an anaesthetist. I was rather hoping to become a Consultant-in-Person (aka a "self-operated patient"). Any tips on that?
Dominic Cooper

Reply

Dominic

The correct name now is a Patient in Person. You will be able to use the hospitals and clog them up so that everyone has to wait much longer for their surgery. There will be a Hospital Admission Fee and that is about to be increased by 600%.

However Hearts R Us, a spin-off from a Valentine's Day flower business, is now operating a no heart no fee deal, which I think might suit you. The key things that you should know are that it will be a florist's assistant performing the surgery and that some of the hearts transplanted are not too fresh, to put it mildly.

Under their Heart to Heart scheme you qualify for a discount if you agree that after 10 years service they can have the heart back unless you pay an additional fee.

Obviously this all used to be done by highly skilled professionals but I am sure you realise that it is much better that companies and their bosses can avoid paying taxes even if that means you have to perform your own heart surgery. What is the point of having a happy, healthy, well- educated secure and safe population if Amazon and Starbucks have to pay tax and put their prices up?

Kerry

Great post …..could be funny if it wasn't actually true !
Hastanton

Yes, this is a problem. Even my most extreme satire is likely to be in a Government White paper the following week……………………

Kerry

74

POOR LAW

A Dick Chilblain Interview!

"Let's get one thing straight" says Tommy Tozzer, "'Poor Law' is not about helping poor people; it is about doing law badly. We wanted to call our ABS "Crap Legal Services" but apparently there is already an ABS with a similar name."

"We want to be the worst, but there is a lot of competition. In the old days you could mark yourself out as really bad by treating clients as conshooomers, never seeing them and just buying and selling them like commodities, but now everyone has cottoned on to that."

Tozzer, 52, who has been involved with many innovative business schemes, said that Poor Law planned to open 1,000 stores with 100,000 TV adverts a day and 10,000 cases and 1,000,000 staff by the end of next month.

"I might not have got all of that right. It is some combination of those round figures. It doesn't really matter. The legal press will print it all."

When Not Lawyers Weekly pointed out that his was the 853rd company in the last 4 weeks to announce its intention to open 10,000,000 law stores this year Tozzer pointed out that, unlike them, he had experience of failing at lots of law related businesses.

"I was at Worsewill and Shidocs and The Accident Waiting to Happen Group. I know more than anyone about screwing up the legal system."

Outside the legal sector Tozzer was involved in an Alternative Dentist Structure where people could upload their own teeth for treatment. However a software mix-up with Onlinebirthing.com, another Tozzer company, resulted in several men with abscesses giving birth and several women in labour having dentures inserted inappropriately.

Tozzer pledged to lose even more money than Co-Op Legal Services and hoped to win awards and be appointed to the government's Law Council.

"The great thing about being rubbish is that there is no limit to your losses. Even the best business can only make £1 for every £1 turnover. We can lose far more than that!"

A spokesman for the Lord Justice Department of Constitutional Chancellors and Affairs Ministers, along with every wannabee lawyer academic, welcomed the move:

"Anything that challenges the system of trained, qualified, insured, disciplined, dedicated professionals is to be welcomed. We have got rid of all professionals in government and now wish to do the same to law, medicine, teaching, the police and the army."

Tommy Tozzer had the last word.

"As the late unlamented Bridgitte Demented said, "There is no reason why buying a tin of baked beans should not be as simple as a Judicial Review application" or something like that."

Not Lawyers Weekly left Tozzer as he was on his way to pick up an award for thinking about opening a billion branches in three days.

LAW'S PARASITES

A Dick Chilblain Special!

Our intrepid reporter catches up with legal entrepreneur Chris Innovator who tells of his life in the law in his own words:

" I started with the protection rackets of the Kray Twins – lovely boys – much maligned- but they got banged up so I moved in to Financial Services – same thing really but less violence.

That got regulated so I became a will-writer flogging dodgy funeral packages. Good one that as the client is always dead when the complaints roll in.

Then Claims Direct and The Accident Group – same thing as the protection rackets but with a bit more violence – but all good things must come to an end. As one door shuts another opens – Claims Management Companies and referral fees and ATE insurance! Those were the days!

Apart from a bit of PPI that is all over. Saw that coming so set up a few Medical Reporting Organisations – MROs – MOR's more like – Money for Old Rope. This Gove chap seems to have sussed that one though, so I've got a few ABS's on the go – they can get away with anything – and do.

Yes, the law has been good to me."

INSTRUCT A LAWYER : A NEW IDEA!

Dick Chilblain reports!

10,000 firms have come up with the idea of people being able to ask them to advise on legal matters and agree a fee to do so!

Being "lawyers" these people will advise on the law; if it is a special matter that needs special help they will ask a specialist to help. The working title for these specialists is "barristers" but some firms prefer the term "counsel".

These "lawyers" have decided to call themselves "solicitors"; they have volunteered to be trained for at least six years, spending about £50,000 on their training.

They will be insured for every penny, and even if the insurance does not cover them for any reason, they will set up and pay for a separate fund, so that no-one can ever lose out.

These "solicitors" and "barristers" will be regulated, at their own expense, and will make themselves subject to all sorts of special rules to protect the public. They plan to call their customers "clients" to mark this difference.

More details will be announced in due course.

Meanwhile a spokesperson for ABS's Past commented:

"What a laugh! It will never catch on. Conshoomers want untrained fly by night businesses likely to go bust to deal with their most important personal and business matters. Discipline, training, regulation,insurance, compensation.What next – ethics, honesty, professionalism?

Namby-pamby nanny-state stuff. No-one will want it. They will be suggesting "courts" as a replacement for sending the boys round. Ridiculous."

GAGA LAW

Dick Chilblain investigates!

GAGA LAW – slogan – The More They Dribble The Less They Quibble – has spotted a gap in the legal market and is seeking to exploit this by becoming an ABS.

The gap is for those lacking capacity or already dead.

Chairman Charlie Cadaver, 132, himself long dead, criticized traditional law firms saying that dead people and those lacking capacity were not catered for.

"Solicitors simply will not take instructions from those lacking capacity. They insist on out of date procedures such as Powers of Attorney and the Court of Protection and such old rubbish. We have a case management system which simply gives us the instructions that the person might have given us if they had capacity. Normally this involves a big fee to us".

Deceased people will be catered for by DeadRight LLP. Partner Christine Corpse, 3½ , said that dead people saw their legacies being squandered and could do nothing about it. Being just 3½ she did not quite put it like that.

Miss Corpse appeared to be unfamiliar with Chapter 2 of the Solicitors Code of Conduct dealing with Equality and Diversity.

Chairman of rival ABS holding company, Drop, Peter Chrysanthemum, who may or may not have been under the influence of a Class A drug, was too busy paying close attention to his laptop to comment, but was later heard singing, to the tune of Lucy in the Sky with Diamonds:

"Picture yourself with a massive great debt

Thirty four pence in the pound

Assets of £3 billion or just forty-seven

Practising law is just hea-ven"

A spokesman for the Solicitors Regulation Authority declined to comment.

A spokesman for the Legal Services Board declined to comment.

A spokesman for the Legal Services Ombudsman declined to comment.

The Coalition Government and Her Majesty's Opposition remain committed to the Legal Services Act.

Other News
On 20 November 2013 a consultation opened on a proposal that would allow the Solicitors Regulation Authority to fine "traditional", that is properly regulated and disciplined, law firms up to £100,000.00, as compared with the current maximum of £2,000.00, that is an increase of five thousand per cent.

Other, Other News
Co-op Legal Services is laying off 60 of its 120 legal staff dealing with personal injury matters.

THE QUEEN'S SPEECH – MAY 2015

Dick Chilblain reports live from Westminster – May 2015

"My previous governments, comprising the Labour, Liberal and Conservative parties have been preparing for the 800th anniversary of Magna Carta. To this end my governments of the last 18 years have: –

- Scrapped legal aid
- Increased court fees tenfold
- Introduced employment tribunal fees causing an 80% reduction in cases
- Heavily restricted Judicial Review
- Allowed non-lawyers to practise law
- Allowed the banks to get away with treason
- Mounted a sustained attack on lawyers and professional people generally
- Introduced damaging and expensive reforms which do not work
- Introduced a further set of damaging and expensive reforms that do not work
- Caused a huge increase in litigants in person clogging up the courts and not getting justice
- Sought to destroy the rule of law
- Acted like a bunch of Nazi yobs towards the legal system.

The fees in my courts are now so expensive that even I cannot afford them and I am the Queen. I am surprised at the tenfold increase in court fees as I spend much of my time giving Royal Assent to endless Bills waffling on about reducing the cost of going to law.

Consequently in exercise of my Royal Prerogative and to celebrate 800 years of Magna Carta I am reversing all of the above changes.

In addition I will never again appoint a Lord Chancellor who is not a lawyer."

Section 4

Miscellaneous Pieces

Miscellaneous Pieces

The following pieces have no particular theme and some are more serious than others.

I will leave you to decide which are serious and which are not, although I have noticed that some of my obviously ironic proposals end up as Government policy!

NATIONAL PRO OH NO! WEEK!

Each year the Law Society promotes National Pro Bono week whereby lawyers work for nothing. Not all of us are keen on the concept.

Yes, it is that time of year again – National Nick What You Want Week, aka National Pro Bono Week.

This year everyone is working for free! It is not just solicitors expected to work for nothing.

Best not to try these until confirmed as they are criminal offences:-

Free petrol!
Just fill up and drive away!

Free shopping!
 Get that supermarket trolley as full as you can and proceed straight to your car! Remember to pay 5p for the bags though.

Travel
Why buy a ticket? Get on that bus or train and have a free trip!

Sports
Just climb over the fence or turnstile. Steal a free programme while you are at it!

Rejected ideas
 The minutes of the National Oh No! Steering Advisory Council Committee Taskforce Thinktank Board show that, unsurprisingly, the following ridiculous – can you believe them?! ideas were rejected:
- Free university education;
- Legal aid;
- Free dental care;
- Free courts;
- Free Employment Tribunals

Meanwhile I set out again an old favourite which is an actual exchange between a person we had had no previous contact with, who surprise surprise, obtained our name from an internet search, and Robert Males, my business partner, who, normally is rather milder mannered that me:-

84

Hello,

are you able to provide free legal representation? I am working, however I am not able to afford solicitors fees.

Thank you

Robert Males' reply

Dear

I thank you for your enquiry.

My firm does not provide free legal representation. If my firm's bank provides interest free loans, my governing body, the Solicitors Regulation Authority, will authorize my firm to practise for free, my firm's professional indemnity insurance is reduced to nil, my firm's staff will all work for nothing, if the computer company who I deal with will provide all computers and servicing free of charge and if the stationery business who we deal with will give us all paper and consumables for free and the utilities will provide gas, electricity and water for free then I may be in a position to provide free representation. Until that time I am not.

My firm does however do a considerable amount of free work for charitable institutions including the Royal British Legion and the Lord's Taverners charity for disadvantaged children as well as making donations to other very good causes.

The only reason that we can do this is because we charge our clients for the very high quality legal advice and work that we do on their behalf.

Yours sincerely

Robert Males

Solicitor

Managing Partner

UNDERWOODS SOLICITORS

In July 2013 fees in Employment Tribunals were introduced. This led to an 80% fall in the number of cases brought by employees who felt that they had been wronged. The two judges in the Administrative Court, part of the High Court, found that there was no evidence that the introduction of fees had led to anyone being able to appeal to bring a claim.

A CHRISTMAS CAROL BY THE HIGH COURT

Scene:
Any solicitor's office in the country (except the Strand).

Solicitor:
So, Ms Peasant you have been sacked because you are pregnant and you have come in for a free interview. Typical of your sort if I may say so.

Client:
It's so unfair. I want to bring a claim. You do no win no fee don't you?

Solicitor:
WE do. The State doesn't. Tribunal fees are £1,200.00 win or lose.

Client:
I haven't got that sort of money! I am unemployed. I've been sacked.

Solicitor:
Come, come now. I am an employment lawyer. I know the minimum wage is £6.50 an hour. Easy to remember; it is one hundredth of what I charge – 200 hours work and you have the fee, unless we need to appeal. Cut out the foreign holidays. Sack the nanny – she won't be able to afford the fee to sue you. My little joke!

Client:
My Mum looks after the children. We only just got by when I was working.

Solicitor:
There I can help you. You need to prioritise your spending. The High Court has said so. Eat your existing children – Swift said that and he was a clever man, but you peasants don't read you just watch Sky.

Client:
We don't have Sky. Murdoch is nearly as right wing as the High Court.

Solicitor:

Go down the library and read Swift.

Client:
They've closed the library.

Solicitor:
Have an abortion. Save you money and I might be able to get your job back.

Client:
I don't want an abortion. Anyway they've closed the clinic.

Solicitor:
Find a rich man.

Client:
I am married. My husband was sacked for complaining about my treatment at work.

Solicitor:
Oh then he has a claim as well then. Another £1,200.00 mind.

Client:
I've had enough!

Solicitor:
I advise on the law; I don't make it. I want to read to you what the High Court said:

"The question many potential claimants have to ask themselves is how to prioritise their spending; what priority should they give to paying fees in a possible legal claim as against many competing and pressing demands on their finances?"

It goes on a bit but basically do you want to bring a claim or eat and feed and clothe your children?

Client:
But no-one should have to make that choice in Britain in 2014.

Solicitor:
That's where you are wrong. The court said:

"The question is not whether it is difficult for someone to be able to pay – there must be many claimants in that position – it is whether it is virtually impossible and excessively difficult for them to do so".

Client:
That's wicked.

Solicitor:
That's the High Court. Lord Justice Elias is paid £198,674.00 and Mr Justice Foskett £174,481.00 so they know all about having to count the pennies.

Client:
Surely Labour will change all this.

Solicitor:
Nope.

Client:
I think I will vote for the Fascists then.

Solicitor:
They tried that in Germany.   Didn't do them much good. Nice rallies mind.

Client leaves. Solicitor hums the Horst Wessel. There is a muffled explosion. The local court is in ruins.

WHO ATE ALL THE PIES?

Fag considered

 The decision of the Court of Justice of the European Communities in Fag Og Arbejde v Kommunernes Landsforening [2014] EU ECJ C-354/13 – 18 December 2014

has been widely misreported. Far from establishing discrimination on the ground of obesity to be unlawful it held that it is not a ground protected from discrimination, that is what in the UK we know as a protected characteristic.

"36. According to the case law of the Court, the scope of Directive 2000/78 should not be extended by analogy beyond the discrimination based on the grounds listed exhaustively in article 1 thereof…"

"37. Consequently, obesity cannot as such be regarded as a ground in addition to those in relation to which Directive 2000/78 prohibits discrimination."

"38. In this case, the file provided to the Court contains nothing to suggest that the situation at issue in the main proceedings, insofar as it relates to a dismissal purportedly based on obesity as such, would fall within the scope of EU Law."

"39. In that context, the provisions of the Charter of Fundamental Rights of the European Union are likewise inapplicable…"

"40. Having regard to the foregoing considerations, the answer to the first question is that EU Law must be interpreted as not laying down a general principle of non-discrimination on grounds of obesity as such as regards employment and occupation."

That is crystal clear and, in contrast to most ECJ judgments, it is in nice, short, crisp paragraphs.

What the court then went on to hold is that obesity could be a disability and of course disability is protected from discrimination and in the UK is a protected characteristic.

That is a very different matter and it is clearly and obviously right. To hold otherwise would effectively deprive a whole group of people from protection. Some people are obese because of medical reasons, or medical treatment, or temporarily because they are pregnant. To exclude from protection those who are obese and to exclude obesity as ever being a disability would, in the UK, class obese people with pyromaniacs, sex maniacs, kleptomaniacs, voyeurs and exhibitionists; those conditions are expressly excluded from being classed as impairments.

Thus in UK law the issue is not whether someone is obese but whether they, put simply, have a long-term impairment. Anything else would be absurd. If a certain level of obesity, and how on earth does one measure that, deprived a person of protection then it may be in employers' interest to fatten up their staff like foie gras geese so as to get the employer off risk.

Would one move in and out of protection depending upon how many beers and curries you had at the weekend?

What is behind this is a feeling that fat people have made a lifestyle choice and have only themselves to blame. That may be true but the disability legislation looks at the consequences of a condition and not its cause.

Are we to stop regarding people with cancer as having a disability if it was caused by smoking? What about the person who is disabled as a result of taking part in dangerous sports? Is diabetes a disability if it is caused by smoking but not if it is caused by being overweight?

As the court here said in a short and lucid paragraph:-

"56. The concept of "disability" within the meaning of Directive 2000/78 does not depend on the extent to which the person may or may not have contributed to the onset of his disability."

That is a perfect and sensible analysis of a sensible law.

The consequences of obesity may be a disability just as the consequences of smoking, the consequences of playing cricket or rugby or parachuting or whatever may be a disability.

The phrase that some commentators have picked up and run with appears at paragraph 64 of the judgment:-

"…the obesity of a worker constitutes a "disability" within the meaning of that directive where it entails a limitation resulting in particular from long term physical, mental or psychological impairment which in interaction with various barriers may hinder the full and effective participation of the person concerned in professional life on an equal basis with other workers."

The suggestion that employers need to provide larger chairs or special car parking and protect employees from verbal harassment in relation to their weight and that shops and cinemas and restaurants must provide bigger seats or special seating arrangements etc is wholly wrong.

I am not always a huge fan of the European Union or of the European Court of Justice. However this is a model decision, short and clear and to the point and very obviously right.

So you can continue singing "Who Ate All the Pies?" and "Have You Ever Seen Your Dick?" without fear of being accused of discrimination.

Notes to the Administrative Court:

1. "Who Ate All the Pies?" and "Have You Ever Seen Your Dick?" are titles of popular songs referring to people's weight and are frequently sung at Association Football matches.
2. Association Football is a popular spectator sport where feckless working class people waste their money instead of saving it for Employment Tribunal fees.

This piece first appeared in Claims magazine issue 23 in February 2016. I am grateful to Claims magazine for permission to use this piece here.

LETTER TO THE EDITOR

Dear Sir

I wonder if any of your readers can help me. I run a small law firm in Hertfordshire and I am not too good with keeping up with the news.

I know that the Chancellorships of the Exchequer and Lord have been combined which is why Mr Osborne now deals with the legal system.

The small claims limit in personal injury is going up to £5,000.00 so that lawyers can only get costs from the other side if the claim is over that amount. That is what Mr Osborne, Member of Parliament for Tatton, said in November but Lord Justice Briggs says we should scrap courts and lawyers for claims under £25,000.00. I can't see which seat he represents in Parliament.

Maybe he took over Lord Justice Jackson's constituency as he does not seem to have been elected to Parliament either. I would just like to know whether the limit is going to be £5,000.00 or £25,000.00 and whether I can represent clients and get costs from the other side, or represent clients and not get costs from the other side or whether I am going to be thrown out of the courts altogether.

Will I be able to get rid of all my insurance and qualifications and professional responsibilities and get paid for being a McKenzie Smart App Friend?

Also I am not sure how lawyers being replaced by Artificial Insemination helps. I am not great with technology and don't want to get into the physical details but how does online Artificial Insemination for cases up to £25,000.00 work? Sounds as though McKenzie needs to become a bit more than a friend.

I have also heard that the Health Minister is bringing in fixed costs for clinical negligence cases but I can't see whether that is for claims up to £25,000.00 or £250,000.00 or when that is coming in.

Apparently clients suffering certain injuries won't be able to claim but I don't know what injuries those are or when it is coming in or how serious the injuries have to be before they can claim. Did I miss some statement by the Minister for Art, Fisheries and Canal Redevelopment dealing with this?

I am glad the Lord Chief Justice wants a 24 hour helpline, Occupational Health and counselling support for us lawyers, although I heard some idiot say that he wanted it for judges and not lawyers. That can't be right! Lord Thomas will never get re-elected to Parliament with views like that! Not sure what constituency he represents.

I think that we should have a separate Government department dealing with all of this – maybe – just throwing a few ideas out – a Lord Chancellors department, or a Ministry of Justice, or something like that so that is can all be thought through.

Apparently there is some book about this by Monty Skew – an Essex boy I believe – but I can't find it on Amazon. I think it is called the Law of Spirits.

Finally is it not time that the insurance companies had a say in all of this? I feel very sorry for them. They have to pay out on all of these claims and no one listens to them.

Yours faithfully

Confused of Hemel Hempstead

(Full name and address supplied)

This piece first appeared in Solicitors Journal in 20 January 2016. I am grateful to Solicitors Journal for permission to use this piece here.

CHANCELLOR'S SPRING 2016 STRATEGY

I am back. Solicitors Journal and I have got back together more times than Richard Burton and Elizabeth Taylor. My first piece is direct from Parliament.

Order! Order! Spring Statement by the Chancellor of the Exchequer

George Osborne

By scrapping general damages and costs in personal injury cases up to a figure that I have not yet determined on a date that I have not yet announced covering types of cases which I have not yet specified I will pass the burden of compensating injured people and treating them from insurance companies to the state.

I had thought that £5,000.00 was the appropriate figure but my friend in the judiciary the Right Honourable Sir Michael Townley Featherstone Briggs, Charterhouse and Magdalene, has advised that we do not need lawyers or courts for any claim under £25,000.00.

The Lord Chief Justice, Lord Thomas (salary £247,112.00) fully supports this and says that the judiciary is suffering from low morale and that their work is not valued or appreciated.

LiPS - Litigious Insolent Plebs – are clogging up the courts so I am abolishing all claims up to £50,000.00. Any above that level will be dealt with on Twitter. To help the morale of the judges - £177,988.00 a year for High Court judges and £202,668.00 for Court of Appeal judges – I am improving their redundancy packages.

As there will be no courts we will not need judges and I am confident that the combination of an index-linked pension, enhanced redundancy packages and no work to do will cheer up the judges.

Your Government has already successfully piloted this scheme in Employment Tribunals where the introduction of unaffordable fees has

94

reduced the workload by 81%. The Administrative Court declined to overrule this move in Judicial Review proceedings and I am glad to have the support of the Senior Judiciary in abolishing courts.

I now turn to the impact statement in relation to road traffic accidents [note to self: pause for laughter] and this shows that the state will lose:-

- CRU recovery
- Court fees
- VAT and income tax and insurance premium tax
- Money in the economy

These costs must be met by savings elsewhere.

Evidence shows that many accidents occur while children are travelling to and from school. This imposes an unacceptable burden on insurance companies and the state so we are closing all schools immediately. Exceptions will be made in relation to Charterhouse, Eton and some others. Closing all schools except public schools is not a decision on ideological grounds. Boarding schools clearly involve less travel and therefore fewer accidents.

I now turn to clinical negligence claims. The cost to the state is unacceptable. I have considered seeking to improve the NHS so that there are fewer deaths and injuries and therefore fewer claims but that is too expensive.

Fixed costs are not the answer as lawyers will find a way of serving their clients just as they did when we reduced portal costs to next to nothing. Unfortunately people still instructed lawyers and courts continued to order negligent people – in reality insurance companies – to pay damages. That cannot continue.

So I am shutting all of the hospitals.

As there will be no mechanism for enforcing laws there is no point in making laws.

Consequently I am shutting Parliament.

"Without lawyers, judges and courts, there is no access to justice and therefore no rule of law, and without the rule of law, society collapses."

Lord Neuberger – Supreme Court President – 10 April 2015

This piece first appeared in Claims Magazine Issue 18 in March/April 2015. I am grateful to Claims magazine for permission to use this piece here.

The Civil Procedure Rules Committee, unelected and unaccountable, drafts the Civil Procedure Rules that is the Rules governing the procedure of the courts in civil litigation.

They are not very good at it.

ALL TOGETHER NOW

Kerry Underwood drops in on the Rules Committee

Member 1: This rule about only getting court fees if you are late wiv your budget. It's mad! The other side can do wot they like – ignore Part 36 and everyfing!

M2: I fink where a naughty party is late but the other party is naughty about Part 36 then as they are both really naughty then the late party should get half.

Chorus: Yeah good idea! Half each if everyone is naughty!

M3: Is it Part 36 cos this is our 36th go at getting it right.

M4: Course it is you muppet. Next time it will be Part 37.

M5: Who made the court fees only rule in the first place?

Chorus: We did stupid! We make mad rules so we can change them.

M7: Let's really muck up Part 36 by making Dodgy Claimant:

Chorus: Over the wall we go – all Claimants are dodgy

M7: by making Dodgy Claimants show that their offers are really,properly,genuinely,madly serious.

Chorus: Yeah! Let's!

M4: Let's muck up the kid's stuff – that really annoys everyone. Let's make them show a risk assessment, even though they won't have one cos your not meant to do it like that now. And let's make them break the law by telling the

97

court the advice they gave to little Johnny. If they don't then no deduction. If they do – contempt of court.

M5: That is in breach of the Act and nearly 1,000 years of common law. It is ultra vires.

Chorus: (to the tune of the Funky Gibbon) *Ooh Ooh Ooh the Ultra Vires*

M5: This is getting out of hand. Thank goodness we got the whole Relief from Sanctions rule spot on. I hate to think what could have happened there, conflicting Court of Appeal decsions, months of chaos, anything.

M3: And proper partiality – that is really good. No-one understands it.

M1: It's called portion penalty, stupid!

Chorus: The sick brown QOCS jumps over the lazy dog.

Kerry left as the Rules Committee started dancing round the room clapping and singing The Birdy Song "with a little bit of this and a little bit of that…."

This piece first appeared in Claims Magazine Issue 19 on May/June 2015. I am grateful to Claims magazine for permission to use this piece here.

KNOCK IT DOWN

In the last issue I imagined what a Civil Procedure Rules Committee Meeting might be like. That was meant to be reasonably light-hearted but things have taken a sinister turn.

The Civil Procedure Rules Committee, unelected, unrepresentative, unaccountable and undemocratic has decided to allow judges to be removed from a whole series of judicial functions including deciding applications in relation to the following matters:-

- amending Particulars of Claim;

- stays

- rectifying procedural errors;

- extending time for service of Claim Form;

- adding or substituting a party;

- making a counterclaim;

- setting aside or varying a default judgment;

- interim payments.

A pilot scheme comes into force on 1 October 2015 and covers claims issued at Northampton Bulk Centre, Money Claims Online and the County Court Money Claims Centre in Salford.

Legal advisers, who must be solicitors or barristers, will now make these decisions which have always been the responsibility of the judges. There will be no hearing.

There has been no consultation about this radical change, which overturns nearly 900 years of judicial matters being determined by judges. No details have been provided as to the training, or more likely lack of training, that these parajudges will receive. There is no minimum period of qualification or call. The parties can within 14 days request a District Judge reconsider the decision. That reconsideration will take place without a hearing.

Now you know what the 622% court fee increase was for.

Remember it is this unbelievably incompetent Civil Procedure Rules Committee which brought you the Relief from Sanctions fiasco, along with virtually unintelligible rules in relation to a whole host of matters including Part 36 and Qualified One-Way Costs Shifting and a complete lack of guidance on matters such as proportionality.

It is time for this subversive bunch of incompetents to be banished and their committee and all its works abolished. Making Civil Procedure Rules should now become a matter for a Parliamentary Committee drawing on the use of experts, that is people who know what they are doing, when needed.

NEXT WEEK: THE CIVIL PROCEDURE RULES COMMITTEE ABOLISHES PARLIAMENT, DECLARES MARTIAL LAW AND RE-WRITES PART 36 FOR THE 83RD TIME

The Civil Justice Council makes proposals concerning the administration of civil justice. It used to be very good.

It no longer is.

SNIVEL INJUSTICE COUNCIL

Candidates required to make futile suggestions concerning the legal system:

Job requirements:

1. You must never have had a proper job.

2. You must never have dealt with a client or member of the public.

3. You most certainly must never have run your own business or taken any commercial risk.

4. You must use the terms "platform", "portal" and "technology" in every paragraph of anything you write.

Personal attributes

1. A willingness to meddle in things you know nothing about.

2. Having a completely safe tax payer funded job with an index-linked pension.

3. Not have any real experience of real life.

This piece first appeared slightly amended in New Law Journal on 13 July 2012 with the title "Turn of Phrase" I am grateful to New Law Journal for permission to use this piece here.

JESUS AND THE TWELVE CONSUMERS

The Legal Ombudsman investigates, and seeks to resolve, complaints about the service provided by lawyers.

In his March 2012 report he states that the term client "embodies the traditional view of the relationship between lawyers and those they represent" and that the "notion of a consumer turns this relationship on its head. In most businesses, the consumer has the power and can choose which services to buy from which provider".

The Ombudsman's suggestion is that many of the perceived problems with lawyers could be solved by a change of name and culture; everything will be fine if we are all consumers, conveniently ignoring the dreadful service that we consumers get from the banks, the utilities, insurance companies etc.

The attempt to turn all clients, patients, pupils, parishioners, passengers, constituents, readers, theatre-goers etc. into consumers is Orwellian. It equates law, medicine, teaching, religion, democracy and the rule of law itself to the equivalent of a packet of cornflakes. For many of us the low point of the last Government was the fatuous statement of the Minister for Justice that obtaining legal advice should be no different from buying baked beans. It is the language of the lowest common denominator.

It is true that the term "client" or indeed "patient" denotes dependency but why should that be considered a bad thing?

Far from being undesirable, surely mutual dependency is the hallmark of a civilized society. One is dependent upon a doctor, one's children are dependent upon teachers, one is dependent upon a pilot when you fly, a plumber when you have a leak etc. What is wrong with that?

The logic of consumerism is each person for him or herself, which is why it is a right-wing concept – think United States of America. Now, there may be a legitimate view that "there is no such thing as society", that there should be no mutual dependency, but rather each person for himself and devil take the hindmost, but will the bleeding-heart brigade please recognize that consumerism is Thatcherite, right-wing ultra-conservative philosophy?

Recently I flew back from Barcelona and the plane hit severe turbulence. The pilot was re-assuring and handled everything superbly and landed us safely. All of us were totally dependent upon him, a trained pilot. I was also glad that I was flying with British Airways and not a budget airline.

Is there any difference between that situation and a trained lawyer guiding a client through the personal storms that life throws up?

Client is a term of respect for the client. Consumer is not; indeed the dictionary definition of "consume" is:

Destroy, occupy or waste time, spend (money or goods) especially wastefully, use so as to destroy; take up and exhaust; use up, eat up, drink down; devour, waste away with disease or grief, decay, rot, burn away

The very language is absurd – imagine – "I must finish this now – I have a consumer waiting".

Law is an art and not a science. Hermann Hesse, in The Glass Bead Game, tells of a society where all art and emotion is reduced to a mathematical formula represented in a three-dimensional glass bead game, and then demonstrates the fallacy of this uber-rational view of human behaviour.

The Legal Ombudsman belittles and demeans the very people he purports to represent. He patronizes them in the way that he thinks that we do.

So, with Easter here, reflect upon the Last Supper and Jesus and his Twelve Consumers.

This piece first appeared in Claims Magazine Issue 5 on 21 December 2012 with the title "A Break in the Link?" I am grateful to Claims Magazine for permission to use this piece here.

MEDIATION IN PERSONAL INJURY: A BAD THING

The Court of Appeal is piloting a mediation scheme for all personal injury and contract claims up to the value of £100,000.00 where permission to appeal has been given.

Known as the Court of Appeal Mediation Scheme (CAMS), it will be managed by the Centre for Effective Dispute Resolution (CEDR), and will run until April 2013.

Parties are expected to mediate unless the judge orders otherwise. If both parties agree to mediate then a panel of accredited CAMS mediators will be nominated by CEDR.

Comment

Mediation in the Court of Appeal is likely to be even less successful, and even more unpopular, than mediation at first instance.

If the case should not be before the Court of Appeal then why was permission to appeal given?

As I have said before mediation is the plaything of those who can afford to pay for litigation twice.

If the case should be before the Court of Appeal then, by definition, the Court of Appeal should hear it, determine it and give guidance for other cases, something that the secretive mediation process singularly fails to do.

Clear Court of Appeal guidance, applicable to all cases, is what saves legal time and money.

Passing the buck to a mediator may appear to save money in a particular case – although rarely does in my experience – but it undoubtedly costs money in uncertainty and wasted costs in other cases.

Yet again it is the relatively low value cases that are being shunted off to the mediator's yard, although £100,000.00 is a huge sum to most people.

Why not start with compulsory mediation for all commercial cases valued over £10 million and see how that goes?

Or, better still, recognize that as a matter of public policy it is wholly unacceptable for matters before the Court of Appeal, where of course, leave has been given, to be forced in to mediation. What possible justification can there be for telling a party who has a judgment of a High Court Judge in its favour that it must now pay for a mediator to look at the case? Why not just endorse all first instance decisions with a message:

"If you have lost you might as well appeal as then your successful opponent will be forced to mediation and if you don't like the result then the Court of Appeal will look at it".

Obviously there will be a dramatic increase in the number of applications for leave to appeal, which will increase, not lessen, costs

The mediation lobby is powerful and vocal and will no doubt cry out that no-one is being forced to do anything. Being told by the Court of Appeal to mediate or face costs penalties is "forcing" in my book.

Parliament, not Judges, should decide what court system we have.

Interestingly Lord Neuberger the new President of the Supreme Court , but speaking when Master of the Rolls, is on record as not being an unqualified supporter of mediation, saying that an insidious notion exists that litigation is a bad thing and that "other, more consensual means of resolving disputes are necessarily good things".

Lord Neuberger said that "access to the courts is not a privilege but a fundamental right", and that if people cannot do that "then justice is either not done or he must resort to violence to achieve a sort of justice. Either way, the rule of law dies. " [1] "A policy which treats the civil justice system merely as a service to be offered at cost in the market place, and to be paid for by those who choose to use it, profoundly and dangerously mistakes the nature of the system and its constitutional function".

Lord Dyson, Master of the Rolls, has said:

"you might be forgiven for thinking that I am not mediation's greatest zealot, and that word: "zealot". It is amazing how it seems to crop up....there is something about mediation which does attract very considerable keenness". [2]

While recognizing the benefits of mediation in certain cases Lord Dyson pointed out that it can be expensive, and if unsuccessful, increases, not lessens costs, and spoke against parties being "frogmarched" to the mediation table and being denied "access to the courtroom".

"Can it be right that a person who has exercised his constitutional right to go to court should be forced to sit down with the individual he believes to have wronged him to try and find a compromise which will probably leave him worse off than he would have been if he had had his day in court?"

He referred to the public interest in the courts promoting "the proper development of the law", a point also recognized by Lord Neuberger who referred to "judges developing the law".

That has now come to a full stop in personal injury cases as all cases are to be shunted off to a second-class, non-judicial, non-binding, secret forum.

Victims of personal injury deserve better than that.

Bentham Lecture 2011
CIArb's Third Mediation Symposium, October 2010

PERSONAL INJURY – A MODEST PROPOSAL

Put the small claims limit in personal injury matters up to £25,000 for matters resolved in the portals but reduce it to zero for all other matters, that is cases that never enter the portal and those that exit the portal.

The recoverable portal costs are almost meaningless now and no solicitor can survive without charging the client. 25% of damages is standard and contrary to popular belief the charge is not limited to 25%.

Let us recognize that and scrap recoverable costs in the portal. This would give defendants an even greater incentive to settle early and reasonably, as otherwise they move from a no-costs regime to a recoverable costs regime.

Clients get their damages quickly and lawyers get their fees quickly. Everybody is happy except those firms who are unable to generate enough work and have to fatten up every file like a pig for market. Those firms need to be driven out.

Increase general damages by 20% to reflect the saving to defendants and to reflect the fact that clients will be paying all of the legal costs out of damages if matters settle early.

A 20% increase in general damages will mean that more money goes to the injured client and we all agree that that is a good thing don't we?

Where the case is low-value but complicated, and this does not go in the portal, for example clinical negligence, the lawyer gets a proper fee, without the fear of an adverse costs order.

Scrap Part 36 for all work in the portals, pendulum litigation and Fixed Recoverable Costs Schemes, bringing them in line with the Small Claims Track where Part 36 has no application.

Scrap Qualified One Way Costs Shifting and make it One Way Costs Shifting.

Limit the consequences of a claimant failing to beat a defendant's Part 36 in any personal injury matter to non-recovery of costs, that is remove the draconian penalty of having to pay the other side's costs, and thus remove the need for After-the-Event insurance. The penalty of not recovering post Part 36 costs is sufficient to incentivize solicitors and clients to accept good offers.

No medical report without leave of the court in any claim worth less than £25,000. In 95% of low-value cases they are unnecessary. Employment

Tribunals deal with the most complex issues such as disability, life expectancy and ability to work, without medical reports.

Pendulum litigation for all personal injury claims up to £50,000 where liability has been admitted and the only issue is quantum.

Pendulum litigation is successfully used in some European jurisdictions. At a quantum hearing each party must submit one figure and the Judge must choose one or the other figure; s/he cannot choose something in between. Thus each party tries to make its figure as reasonable as possible to ensure that that is the figure that the Judge goes for. We have the beginnings of that in the portal system; now is the time to go the whole hog. It works.

All personal injury claims not settled by way of a Settlement Agreement or in the Pendulum Litigation process to be dealt with in a new Personal Injury Tribunal. This will be chaired by a Judge sitting with two lay assessors, very much based on the old, successful Employment Tribunal system.

There would be a system of one way Fixed Recoverable Costs with the defendant only able to recover costs in the event of unreasonableness as in the Employment Tribunal Rules.

There will be no court fees and the lay assessors will consist of one from the claimant side and one from the insurance side, again based on Employment Tribunals where there was a trade union nominated tribunal member and an employer organization nominated member.

It is striking in the Employment Tribunal system how rarely there is a split decision. A similar system in personal injury work may help to end the deeply damaging "them and us" culture that has grown up between the claimant side and the defendant side.

Appeal, with leave, will be direct to the Court of Appeal, which would be a costs-free zone in accordance with powers under the new CPR 52.9A.

Cases must be determined on paper within 14 days of notification to the Personal Injury Tribunal that liability has been admitted. There would be a right of appeal, but the Appeal Judge would still have to choose one or other figure. (Those of you who have attended my lectures will have seen my party piece on this).

Clinical Negligence
A no fault scheme, that is where proof of injury cause by medical treatment is sufficient with no need to prove negligence.

This would not risk opening the floodgates, and given the enormous budget of the NHS, and its 1.7 million employees, extra payments to compensate those injured, whether or not it was anybody's fault, makes no noticeable financial difference.

In any event society often ends up, through the benefit system, paying out in respect of people severely injured through medical treatment.

A new, Specialist Clinical Negligence Tribunal, along the lines of the Personal Injury Tribunal above would deal with matters, that is essentially decide quantum.

Allow out and out contingency fee agreements in all personal injury work, and indeed in all civil work.

Scrap Damages-Based Agreements. Pointless and useless. Contingency fee agreements and Conditional fee agreements do the job. CMCs are currently allowed to enter in to DBAs, which is wholly wrong. This does away with that anomaly.

This can be achieved by amending Section 57(2) of the Solicitors Act 1974 which already allows contingency fee agreements in non-contentious business, and by the repeal of section 45 of the Legal Aid, Sentencing and Punishment of Offenders Act 2012 and the consequent scrapping of the Damages-Based Agreements Regulations 2013.

Careful drafting of a section 57(2) agreement and a bridging agreement allied to a concurrent Conditional Fee Agreement allows this to be achieved anyway.

A maximum percentage of damages to be charged to the client should be introduced, maybe 30% in personal injury work and 40% in clinical negligence work, such percentages to include everything to be charged to the client with recovery of costs from the other side to continue in the circumstances set out above.

Contrary to popular belief the current law does not impose any limit on the percentage to be charged to the client; it is merely the percentage to be charged by way of a success fee or DBA that is limited.

Scrap the indemnity principle. It is the single biggest cause of the increase in legal costs. There is no logical reason why recovery should be limited to the notional charge to the client. Conditional fee agreements have rendered it almost meaningless anyway.

Reduce limitation period to six months. If you haven't lodged a claim in six months then it could not have troubled you much. Make this subject to existing Limitation Act exceptions.

Extend system of Interim awards as per portals.

Ban ABSs from dealing with personal injury work – qualified lawyers only.

Ban Claims Management Companies from having any involvement of any kind in personal injury work. Referral fees in personal injury work are now banned so what justification is there for the continued involvement of CMCs in personal injury work?

Allow barristers direct access in personal injury matters.

Amend Compensation Act to provide for 2 year prison sentence for paying or receiving referral fees, in line with other Compensation Act offences.

Full details of all cases issued should be available to everyone online, with all decisions to be published electronically and on Twitter the day that they are given. This would introduce "Sunshine in Litigation" and works well in those states of the United States where it operates.

Unsolicited telephone calls or text messages soliciting claims to be punishable with a six month prison sentence.

No fee to be recoverable from the other side if a qualified lawyer has not physically met with, and advised, the client.

If this has not happened then the client should be treated as a litigant in person.

The diversity and independence of the legal profession should be encouraged and promoted and the statist big-business mentality that is wholly inappropriate in relation to the practice of law should be discouraged. To help with this, the limit on partnerships must be reintroduced, but perhaps now at 30, rather than 20, with a 25 per cent fee enhancement on Fixed Recoverable Costs for firms with five or fewer partner, and for barristers who should have direct access in all personal injury matters.

Third Party Capture and Settlement Agreements

No personal injury claim of any kind to be settled without the injured party taking advice from a qualified, insured lawyer.

Thus any settlement direct between a claimant and an insurance company will be non-binding unless supported by a Settlement Agreement where the claimant has been advised by a solicitor, Fellow of the Chartered Institute of Legal Executives or a barrister. No paralegals here please; this is sufficiently important to justify qualified lawyers only. Barristers should be allowed direct access for the purpose of dealing with Settlement Agreements.

This is exactly what happens in employment matters and for the same reason, that is to prevent exploitation of the weaker party in an unequal relationship – see section 203 Employment Rights Act 1996.

Settlement Agreements in employment work exceptionally well. As the signing of the agreement and payment of the damages, after the receipt of qualified legal advice, debars the claimant from going to court the custom has grown up of the defendant/respondent employer paying the claimant's legal costs, even though there is no obligation to do so, employment tribunals generally being costs-free zones.

In employment matters the usual fee in a straightforward case is £350.00 plus VAT. For personal injury the appropriate fee may be £750.00 plus VAT, payable by the insurers.

The benefit to the client is very rapid settlement with no deduction from damages. Insurers get the matter off their books at a reasonable cost without the risk of the matter exiting the portal to Fixed Recoverable Costs. It will also cover all non-portal matters, such as clinical negligence.

Quick settlement for the claimant without deduction of damages; reasonable fee for proper lawyers. We are all in favour of that aren't we?

These are some initial, uncontroversial proposals which I am sure will attract general agreement and I would welcome some more radical proposals from readers :)

SOLICITORS REGULATION AUTHORITY AND THE £250 MILLION FINE

In November 2013 the <u>Solicitors Regulation Authority</u> issued a <u>consultation paper</u> where it sought power to increase its maximum fine on solicitors' firms from £2,000 to £250 million.
I have not made that up.

The logic is that £250 million is the maximum fine that the SRA can impose on an Alternative Business Structure (ABS), this figure having been set by the overarching regulator the Legal Services Board. The maximum fine on an individual is £50 million.

These are extraordinary and absurd figures given that punishment by the SRA, as compared with a referral to the Solicitors Disciplinary Tribunal, is meant to be "a considerably quicker, cheaper and more proportionate regime for levying fines."

Quite what aspect of a £250 million fine is proportionate to anything escapes me. This is Jackson-Mitchell on steroids.

Apparently increasing the maximum fine to £250 million "could save considerable time, stress and cost for regulated persons". Personally, and I may be at odds with my colleagues here, I find the prospect of being fined £250 million more, not less, stressful, than being fined £2,000, but that might just be me being quirky.

The worrying aspect is the wish to impose financial penalties "in-house" to use the SRA's wording, that is as an administrative, rather than a judicial process. It is the equivalent of a Fixed Penalty notice for a minor traffic offence, except that the proposed penalty would wipe out all but a very few of the biggest firms.

The proposed maximum fine for an individual is £50 million. Putting aside the stereotypical jokes about the earnings of lawyers is there a single lawyer in England and Wales who has amassed so much from the law that they could afford such a sum? That would have meant saving £1.25 million after tax each year in a 40 year career.

The argument is that the SRA already has these powers in relation to Alternative Business Structures. These limits were set by the Legal Services Board under the provisions of the Legal Services Act 2007. That begs the question of whether those figures for ABSs are appropriate.

It also misses the point that the potential nature of ABSs – huge multi-national companies – led to these very high potential penalties. At Paragraph 32 of the consultation paper the SRA says:

"One point that has been made to us by some stakeholders in the context of our proposal to seek commensurate fining powers is that higher penalties are necessary within the ABS regime because ABSs are of higher means or may be less deterred from misconduct by the prospect of being removed from future legal practice than a solicitor would".

It then rejects that analysis, pointing out that some ABS are small and of moderate means. Quite how that justifies a massive increase in fining powers for solicitors' firms, rather than a reduction in fining powers in relation to small ABSs, is beyond me.

Interestingly the highest fine ever imposed by the Solicitors Disciplinary Tribunal, which has unlimited fining powers, is £50,000.

The consultation paper is useful in that it provides some facts about the powers of the various regulatory bodies and the penalties imposed.
I have been qualified for 33 years but I must admit to having no idea of the punitive role of the Legal Services Ombudsman as compared with the SRA and the SDT and the overlap between the matters the Ombudsman can investigate and those that the SRA deals with. I still don't. However the fining powers over solicitors are:

Ombudsman: £50,000

SRA: £2,000

SDT: unlimited

Only the SDT can suspend or strike-off a solicitor.

Crucially the SDT generally applies the criminal standard of proof whereas the SRA applies the civil standard and the Ombudsman is not bound by any legal principles.

At the very beginning of its consultation the SRA says that it "is the independent regulatory body of the Law Society of England and Wales. We protect the public by regulating law firms and individuals who provide legal services".
Fair enough, but it is crucial to recognize that the job of lawyers is also to protect the public, often against the State and its manifestations, as well as big business.

113

Driving small and medium sized firms out of business through massive fines, or the threat of massive fines, harms, rather than protects, the public. It is the small and medium-sized firms who do most to protect the public, rather than big business.